MORE INSTANT SELF HYPNOSIS

"hypnotize yourself
as you read"

FORBES ROBBINS BLAIR

Author of:

Instant Self Hypnosis
Self-Hypnosis As You Read
Self-Hypnosis Revolution
The Manifestation Manifesto
The Manifestation Matrix
The Manifestation Mindset
The Manifestation Revelation
The Manifestation Trilogy

Edit & Design by Rob Morrison

Forbes Robbins Blair

New Creations Publishing
Gaithersburg, Maryland

The Manifestation Revelation

Copyright © 2011 Forbes Robbins Blair

4th edition, March 2017

All rights reserved under International and Pan-American Copyright Conventions.

No part of this book may be reproduced in any form or by any electronic or mechanical means including information by storage retrieval systems—except in the case of brief quotations embodied in critical articles or reviews—without permission in writing from the publisher.

This publication is designed to provide accurate and authoritative information for the subject matter covered. It is sold with the understanding that the publisher and author is not engaged in offering medical or psychological treatment or professional advice. If you need professional services, please seek the services of a competent professional.

www.forbesrobbinsblair.com

CONTENTS

CONTENTS..v
WHY YOU SHOULD READ THIS BOOK......................1
INTRODUCTION..5
CHANGE YOUR MIND, CHANGE YOUR LIFE...........11
HYPNOSIS ESSENTIALS...19
HOW I DISCOVERED THE "EYES-OPEN METHOD" 31
YOUR FIRST SESSION..35
   "Master Induction 2.0"...41
48 HYPNOSIS SCRIPTS..47
BODY, HEALTH & SEXUALITY SCRIPTS..................53
   "Become More Attractive"......................................55
   "Curvy, Slim Body"..57
   "Easy Weight Release"..61
   "Eliminate Warts"...65
   "Feel Sexy"..67
   "Feminine Pleasure"..71
   "Firmer, Lasting Erections"...................................75
   "Go to the Gym"..79
   "Good Posture"...83
   "Healthy Choices, Healthy Body"..........................87
   "Increase Metabolism, Burn More Calories".......91
   "Love Low Carb Eating".......................................95
   "Reduce Hot Flashes"...99

"Reduce Stress and Blood Glucose Levels".......... 103
"Relieve Chronic Back Pain"................................. 105
"Strong, Lean and Powerful Body" 107
MIND, BEHAVIOR & SPIRIT SCRIPTS...................... 111
"Achieve My Potential".. 113
"Assertive, Confident Salesperson"....................... 117
"Astral Travel Tonight" 121
"Attract a Mate"... 125
"Attract Surplus Money".. 129
"Become a Leader"... 133
"Better Golf Score"... 139
"Brighten Your Aura".. 139
"Deeper Voice" 141
"Emotion Control" 145
"Find Misplaced Objects" 149
"Forgivenesss".. 157
"Get Out of Bed in the Morning"............................ 157
"Honoring Your Feminine Self" 161
"Job Interview Confidence" 163
"Joyful Living".. 167
"Lighten Up!"... 171
"Lucky Me!"... 175
"More Faith in the Divine" 177
"Neat Freak".. 179
"Okay to Be Gay".. 181
"Overcome Alcohol".. 185
"Overcome Depression" 189
"Overcome Fear of Failure" 193

"Reduce Smoking Easily" 197
"Remember Past Lives" 201
"Smile!" 205
"Stay in the Now" 209
"Stop Complaining, Stop Gossiping" 211
"Stop People Pleasing" 215
"Stop Smoking Finally!" 219
"Stop Worrying" 223
BONUS SECTION 225
ENHANCE SCRIPT IMPACT 227
DEEPER INSTANT SELF-HYPNOSIS 229
   "Super Deepening Script" 239
   "Ultra-Deepeneing Script" 241
RAPID INDUCTION 235
   "Rapid Induction Script" 237
INSTANTLY HYPNOTIZE OTHERS 239
   "Modified Master Induction 2.0" 241
EVERYDAY SELF-HYPNOSIS 245
QUESTIONS 251
ABOUT 255
REVIEW 257
BOOKS+ 259
THANK YOU 269
NOTES 271

WHY YOU SHOULD READ THIS BOOK

MOST OF US SPEND EACH DAY searching for ways to get more out of life. Suzanne wants to find a way to manage her diabetes naturally by controlling her blood sugar levels. Pete wants to stop people pleasing and become a leader. Brenda feels she needs to lose that post-pregnancy belly fat. Ting-ting wants to gain confidence for job interviews. Joe wants to have a stronger, leaner body. Kristin needs to smile more and worry less.

Most people want to take away the negative and move toward the positive. They want change but they do not have the right tools to make that happen.

The truth is that most people are busy and it can be tough to find time for self-improvement because so many things pull at us from every direction. We lose focus because of the distractions of the internet, texting, cable television, fighting traffic
and working too-many-hours-to-make-busy-ends-meet. It is no wonder we feel stressed and make choices that sometimes lead to poor habits.

The essential point is that most self-improvement methods require too much time and effort for us to put into practice. Even when we do find the time and wherewithal to reach for change, the techniques we implement often fail to deliver.

Fortunately, you have a proven solution in your hands right now! This book provides a surprisingly fast, workable, and effective way to make good habits easy to acquire.

It only requires only about 15-20 minutes a day for a few consecutive days to experience those changes. There will be no hour-long sessions. No memorization or recording of hypnosis scripts. No listening to hypnosis audios. No complicated solutions. You just read to succeed.

The process is easy. First, you read a script that hypnotizes you as you read. Once you are hypnotized, you read another script with powerful post-hypnotic suggestions related to your goal. To finish, you read a script that safely brings you back to everyday awareness. Then you watch as the improvements show up automatically in your daily life.

Within a few sessions of the hypnosis-as-you-read technique, you can make authentic and measurable changes that astound you.

This is not an empty promise. Thousands of people all over the world have used this method to lose weight, stop smoking, gain confidence, manage their stress and many other goals. You can read their testimonials online. This technique can work for you also!

What would it mean for you to "Reduce Smoking Easily" or to "Stay in the Now" or to "Attract Surplus Money"? Included are 48 goal scripts that cover a wide range of topics. You can start working with them in just a little while from now if you keep reading.

Many hypnosis textbooks explain the history, science and mechanics of hypnosis and self-hypnosis. However, this is not a textbook. It is a practical book.

You will succeed,

Forbes Robbins Blair

PS—Brenda, one of my readers, sent an email the day after she bought this book. She explained her situation to me, and after telling me her doubts ("I don't usually succeed with self-help books.") she asked what she could do to make this time different.

Here is my reply:

The Manifestation Revelation

Hi Brenda!

*Thanks for writing to me.
I understand you are worried about reaching your goals. Let me address that...*

Someone once said that when the only tool you have is a hammer every problem tends to look like a nail. Forget that kind of thinking. Just trust that eyes-open self-hypnosis will work for you, and relax a about the results.

For each of your hypnosis sessions, resolve to do that session at the same time of day for consecutive day, enjoy the journey and have fun.

Also, take positive action steps by sharing your plan to do this with someone supportive. Believe in your potential to be more successful starting today. In other words:

** Believe in Your Potential
* Devise a Plan
* Act*

I know you can do this, Brenda!

—Forbes

INTRODUCTION

ONE DAY IN 1997, while I was reading a hypnosis script designed to hypnotize a client, I accidentally hypnotized myself with my eyes open! The experience was so incredible I decided to experiment with it as a workable self-hypnosis technique for my practice.

The results were impressive. In fact, they far exceeded those of traditional self-hypnosis methods. Among other things, I used the technique to help me successfully lose excess body fat, to stop procrastinating about growing my business and to reduce my pollen allergies.

It worked better than the hypnosis scripts and audios I had tried. I knew I was on to something extraordinary.

Traditional self-hypnosis methods had often failed to keep my concentration from wavering. I even fell asleep during some of those sessions.

With this eyes-open method, my attention was sharp and focused. In addition, it was easy to stay awake and involved.

I knew that many of my clients and colleagues shared my difficulties with traditional methods. I asked them to test my hypnosis-as-you-read technique. Their results were so dramatic it encouraged me to share my findings with a larger audience.

I began to teach eyes-open hypnosis at adult learning centers and at various self-improvement seminars. As the number of satisfied eyes-open hypnosis enthusiasts snowballed, I thought, "Why not make it available to people all over the world as a book?"

That was how I was inspired to write my first book, *Instant Self-hypnosis: How to Hypnotize Yourself with Your Eyes Open* (called "ISH" for short), which became a bestseller and has been translated into several languages. People from all over the United States, England, Russia, Germany, France, Australia, India, New Zealand, and Japan have contacted me to tell me how much the method improved their lives. The emails I continue to receive are wonderful testimonies to its simplicity and effectiveness.

Eyes-Open Hypnosis Method Overview

The method requires no prior knowledge of self-hypnosis whatsoever. You merely set aside a block of 15-20 minutes each day for a few consecutive days to conduct brief but powerful eyes-open self-hypnosis sessions.

The sessions involve a three-step process:

1. You sit down in a private place and read a script that hypnotizes you with your eyes open, called the "Master Induction 2.0."

2. You remain hypnotized as you then read a script of your choice pertaining to your goal or challenge. This script contains a series of carefully worded suggestions that target your inner mind to manifest positive change.

3. To return to your usual safe consciousness and efficiency you read the "The Wake-Up" script included at the end of each goal script.

> *You choose your goal, apply the hypnotic induction and suggestion script, and*

*return safely and gently to your
usual state of mind.*

How to Use this Book

In the first three chapters, I lay out the essential information about self-hypnosis, how I discovered the eyes-open method and I present brief hypnotic experiments that condition you for future success.

I have had people who attend my classes and seminars undergo the same experiments. They have found them worthwhile, fun, and easy to do. You will too.

Next, you will be encouraged to hypnotize yourself with your eyes open as you read the Master Induction 2.0. It is an improved version of the original 2004 Master Induction. I recommend 2.0 to everyone—new and readers of ISH alike. It works faster and is more effective than the 2004 version.

Chapter 5 contains 48 scripts with a wide variety of topics. You will use them together with Master Induction 2.0 to reprogram your inner mind to reach your goals. Each of the 48 goal suggestion scripts helps you establish new ways of thinking, feeling, and behaving that will dramatically improve your quality of life in specific ways. Although the original *Instant Self Hypnosis: How to Hypnotize Yourself with Your Eyes Open* scripts for smoking cessation and weight loss have been successful for many readers, I have included fresh, effective versions of those goals here as well. They are "new and improved."

Toward the end of this book is a Bonus Section with these features and benefits:

* A way to enhance the impact of the suggestions

* Two deepening scripts for those who want to experience advanced, profound alternatives to the basic versions.

* A script to enter the hypnotic state even faster

* A modified induction to hypnotize other people easily

* A special technique that uses your everyday activities to catapult you to your success

* Answers to your popular questions about the "eyes-open hypnosis" method

What is Not Included in This Book

This book does not contain information about how to create your own eyes-open scripts. That material is covered in my first book, *Instant Self Hypnosis: How to Hypnotize Yourself with Your Eyes Open*.

Before You Begin

Before you start to work on your specific goal, it is highly recommended that you read the opening chapters. They are essential if you are new to the method and will ensure your success.

They are brief and, before you know it, you will be able to put the method to work. They contain a hypnotic structure to help you get the most out of the method. Do not skip them.

The opening chapters in this book prepare you for success. They are worth reading.

However, if you are already familiar with the principles of the method (from having read my book, *Instant Self Hypnosis*), you may skip the first three chapters and proceed directly to Chapter 4 where you will find a new and improved induction (Master Induction 2.0) and the important introductory instructions.

Whether you are new to this method or a seasoned and satisfied user, I predict you will be pleased and excited about what I have prepared for you. When you experience the benefits from

More Instant Self Hypnosis, I would love to hear about it. Let me know how you have improved and enhanced your life, if you wish.

CHANGE YOUR MIND, CHANGE YOUR LIFE

IN THIS CHAPTER, YOU WILL LEARN how your mind has its own filtering system that works well—until you want to change a longstanding behavior or belief.

You will also learn why self-hypnosis provides such an excellent way to reach your goals.

A Battle in Your Mind

Your mind is a wonderfully complex system with different levels that have unique functions. However, there can sometimes seem to be a battle going on regarding your behavior and which part of your mind wins in the War of Habits.

That is because there are two parts of your mind: the conscious mind and another part called the subconscious mind. They usually work in harmony. However, there are times when their functions interfere with one another and seem to work against each other.

The conscious mind handles your waking awareness, your observations, and your analysis of life events. Then it calculates and decides how to solve the problems that bother you in the moment. It makes decisions to get you through your day such as, "Do I want to eat cereal or eggs for breakfast?", "Should I wear the red outfit or the blue one today?" or "Should I tell my boss what I really think of him?"

You could think of the conscious mind as the objective or "rational" mind because it offers reasons why you do things. It bases them on concepts you have previously learned and accepted, even when they are false or wrong. This often activates a defense mechanism called rationalization where we justify an attitude or behavior that would otherwise be unacceptable. Instead of coming to grips with our own errors and lapses in logic, we rationalize our decisions and behaviors. It is a typical thing most people do.

Here is an example of rationalizing. Some people come up with all sorts of "logical" reasons they continue to smoke even though they know it is hazardous to their health. They say it calms them or that it keeps them from eating too much. They say the reason they do not quit smoking cigarettes is that they "know" how "difficult" and "addictive" cigarettes are. Their conscious minds cling to those rationalizations and they remain stuck in that habit.

They rarely stop to consider whether there might be other reasons why they continue to smoke. Often one of the real reasons they smoke is that when they first started, it helped them fit in with a group of peers. They conditioned themselves (unknowingly, for the most part) to smoke to tap into that sense of security all over again. It is not really smoking a cigarette that makes them feel good; it is their associations with the smoking activity.

Breaking through those rationalizations can be a challenge. They can start by questioning their justifications for the bad habit. For instance, when I see smoking cessation hypnosis clients I point out that nicotine is a stimulant, which does not calm them at all. When they tell me how hard it is to stop, I mention that I have had many clients who stopped smoking while they experienced no withdrawal symptoms or weight gain. In addition, I offer insight into the emotional connection with smoking and how there are ways to feel safe and secure without cigarettes.

Exposing rationalizations in this nonjudgmental way and then suggesting healthy alternatives usually clears the way for positive change.

By the way, do not feel bad if you are a smoker who feels locked into that behavior. All people have rationalizations for unhealthy or undesirable behaviors at one time or another. Smoking is just one of the more common habits.

To free yourself of the desire for any other unwanted behavior, it is first helpful to understand how your mind has fooled you into staying stuck. It is time to get honest.

Experiment—
"Recognize Your Rationalizations. Your First Step"

Think for a moment about an undesirable behavior pattern and see if you can find any rationalizations that have you justifying that habit. What reasons do you have for staying stuck? Are those reasons verifiably true or false rationalizations in disguise?

Then ask yourself, "Do I want to stop or change this behavior?" Be honest with yourself, as this is your first important step.

Another influence of the conscious mind is what people refer to as *willpower*. You already know about it. You use willpower to make every decision throughout your day.

When it has come to changing a *longstanding* behavior, you might have felt you were in a tug of war with that willpower.

One part of you might have said, "I'm going to only have two or three French fries and let the rest go." Another part of you said, "Yum. Fries taste good." And before you could blink, you ate all the fries! Some other part of your mind impaired your conscious willpower—a part with tremendous influence on your decision-making.

That is why it can be difficult to "will" a habit away or strong-arm yourself into a new way of doing things. While it can be done, it is usually a tough fight and difficult to win.

Can you guess with which part of your mind you have tug of war battles like this? You guessed it—the *subconscious*. The subconscious mind (also called the *unconscious* mind) is a very powerful part of your mind. It runs most of your body's functions without your conscious mind's assistance. It stores and accesses all your habits, emotions, beliefs, memories, and preferences. It is like an infinitely complex computer that you have been programming since you were born, cataloging all your life's experiences and reactions to them. In fact, as you read this you are adding to its programming.

The problem we face when we try to change a habit, belief, or preference by using the powers of the conscious mind is that the old software is still running beneath the surface and out of reach. Willpower is usually insufficient to override the old programming.

Sometimes we can carry it off for a while. But we usually return to our old ways of doing things because our subconscious mind holds on to the imagery that keeps us anchored to those familiar patterns of thought and behavior.

True change usually has little to do with applying willpower all by itself. It must do with correctly directing the power of your *subconscious imagination* with tools like self-hypnosis.

*The subconscious mind
responds to imagery.*

Here is an example. Let us get back to those calorie-heavy fries. Many of us have unknowingly programmed ourselves to imagine how delicious and satisfying it would be to taste and swallow a French fry. Because the anticipated pleasure of eating more fries is more appealing and rewarding than stopping at just two or three fries, our old programming tells us to keep eating them!

*Whatever dominantly appeals to your
subconscious imagination exerts great
influence over your behavior.*

There is always a reason you do what you do, even if you are consciously unaware of your motivations. Your subconscious mind steers you toward pleasure or away from pain.

To avoid pain, the subconscious part of your mind automatically attempts to protect you from some real or imagined danger, often quite successfully. It does this automatically, without conscious consent or intention.

Unless we *change that image-based programming* and get our subconscious to imagine different and better things, our habitual behaviors are unlikely to remain changed for very long. Using direct conscious willpower by itself is a poor way to reprogram the subconscious imagination. Happily, there is a better way.

Reprogramming Yourself Made Easy

I know of no faster or easier way to reprogram the subconscious than through self-hypnosis.

Self-hypnosis bypasses the critical mechanism of the mind and stablishes a condition of heightened suggestion.

Again, your mind's computer security system prevents you from tampering with its inner programming and creating chaos. This is the critical and analytical part of the conscious mind. You should welcome this security system because without it, you would respond to every idea and suggestion that came to you and your life would be in total confusion.

Here is a metaphor to help you understand how self-hypnosis can end this war of habits. When we want to present requests and ideas to the subconscious, the self-critical part is like a security guard standing faithful watch at the doorway to a luxurious mansion. Self-hypnosis provides a way to relax and distract the security guard for short periods of time so we can slip inside to make changes using specific suggestions. When we are finished delivering those messages, we just leave the way we came restoring our security guard to full alertness and just go about our business. The positive habits then show up automatically because we reprogrammed the subconscious with self-hypnosis to agree with our conscious intentions.

Going back to a previous example, we could use hypnotic suggestions when we confront that plate of fries. We could get our subconscious to picture and feel the rewards of a flat stomach when we limit ourselves to just two or three of them. That way, we would no longer even want to eat more than three fries at a time—much less the whole plate.

No tug-of-war with your willpower. Your conscious and subconscious parts of your mind would be in perfect alignment.

True Story—
"How False Rationalizations Nearly Derailed One Woman's Weight Loss Attempts"

Carole was my hypnosis therapy client who had gained 50 pounds over the last couple of years.

Her rationalization for that was she was in a "change of life" and that weight loss is a natural consequence of those hormonal changes.

To help understand how she gained that much body fat, I asked her to recall when she first started gaining weight and whether anything significant had changed in her life. She told me she had just gotten divorced. I asked if she wanted to marry again. She said "yes" but she still feared the possible pain of getting divorced again.

I believe her subconscious was trying to protect her from experiencing future pain by allowing those layers of fat to accumulate. That way, she would make herself less appealing to men and avoid the possibility of another marriage ending in divorce!

Once she understood how her rationalizations were keeping her stuck and covering up the truth, it became easy to apply hypnosis effectively to lose those 50 pounds.

Easily Change Habits with Self-hypnosis

Self-hypnosis can help you change an unlimited number of personal habits.

This is not limited to behavioral habits or emotional changes. Self-hypnosis can help you change your physical body too!

This surprises many people. However, remember that the subconscious controls most of your body's functions like the organs, hormones, and cells? It can work to improve your body in many ways.

When the subconscious is reprogrammed through hypnotic suggestions with imagery like: "...safely and incrementally raise the metabolism to burn more calories..." your subconscious mobilizes your body's resources to make it a reality.

You might be wondering just how this is done. However, just as it is unnecessary to understand how your laptop computer sends emails or runs installed applications, it is not important to understand the science of how the mind works on you through hypnotic suggestion.

Your subconscious fully understands your body, and it knows how to alter its functions. Tell it what you want with tools like self-hypnosis. Then, it will use its deep resources to make those changes you want happen!

True Story—
(Warning: Not for the Squeamish)

I had a 45-year-old client named Craig who was addicted to a popular candy bar. He ate six king-sized bars every day with his coffee and gained 35 pounds of body fat! He came to me for help.

His situation was extreme and his personality was resistant, He needed a more exaggerated form of hypnotherapy. With his approval, I reprogrammed his subconscious imagination to make a correlation between the general length, shape, and color of the brown candy bar and (how do I put this delicately?) ... well ... feces. This is an "aversion suggestion".

For Craig, this approach proved quite effective. After that session, he never again had the slightest interest in eating candy bars. In fact, the sight of candy bars disgusted him.

HYPNOSIS ESSENTIALS

YOU ARE PROBABLY EXCITED to put the suggestion scripts to work. But read this chapter first because it is going to help you maximize your results.

Who's Afraid of Hypnosis?

When you think of hypnosis, what images come to your mind? A swinging watch? A spinning spiral? An entertainer controlling people to perform strange or embarrassing things on stage? These clichés, perpetuated by some people, have led many to believe that hypnosis is weird, humiliating, or dangerous.

> *Therapeutic hypnosis is
> very different though.*

Hypnosis has come a long way over the last several decades. Today, few professional hypnotherapists use the tools of carnival hypnotists and antiquated devices like dangling watches or spirals to hypnotize people. There are much better techniques.

Stage hypnotists are all about entertaining the audience. Just as a stage magician does magic tricks, a great deal of the stage hypnotist's effectiveness relies on illusion and deception. His participants really are in control always, and they can hear and remember everything. They just choose
to participate in the fun and do what the hypnotist suggests—if he does not ask them to do something humiliating or dangerous.

Everyone has a natural morality-based off-switch for those situations—no matter how deeply hypnotized they may be.

To understand therapeutic hypnosis better, here are some points to note:

* *Hypnosis does not make you lose control.* It does not make you want to tell secrets or do anything you find offensive, embarrassing, or dangerous. Every person has her/his own protective inner moral compass.

* *Hypnosis is not magic, nor is it a trick.* Hypnosis is an authentic mental phenomenon where you are in a state of heightened suggestibility—with your approval. It is not a hoax. It is not super-natural.

* *Hypnosis is not sleep.* During hypnosis, you are awake always. Many hypnotists use phrases like "You are getting sleepy" just to relax the participant's body and mind. Alternately, some use the command to "Sleep!" as a pre-determined cue for a willing person to enter hypnosis quickly. However, this does not refer to actual sleep.

* *Hypnosis does not automatically result in amnesia.* Unless someone decides to accept a suggestion to "forget" some part of a hypnosis session, it is unlikely she or he would forget. People hear everything and remember everything when the hypnosis session is finished. It is stored in their subconscious to be used later.

* *No one becomes "stuck" in hypnosis.* Hypnosis is a natural condition from which a person comfortably emerges. There is no danger of being stuck in the hypnotic state.

Hypnosis does not feel strange. For most people, hypnosis is a subtle experience. Some people do not even know they are hypnotized because it feels natural.

Experiment—
"What Hypnosis Feels Like"

Want to know what hypnosis might feel like? Try this little experiment. Go ahead and try it now...

"Put your feet flat on the floor. Draw a slow deep breath, and as you exhale, close your eyes, relax and count from one to five. Then open your eyes and keep reading."

Did you follow the instructions exactly? You probably did not feel anything yet. Still, you decided to obey my suggestions because you want to get something out of this book. Also, you figure the best way to do that is to follow instructions here.

Try it again please...

"Make sure your feet are flat on the floor. Get comfortable. Draw a slow, deep breath, and when you exhale relax deeper. Think the words 'hypnosis now' as you close your eyes and count to five. Then, open your eyes and continue to read. Do it when you are ready.

"Now, quack aloud like a duck! "Go ahead. Quack three times aloud. I mean it!"

Did you quack?
If not, why not? Let me guess: Because it would seem "silly"?
On the other hand, if you did quack, why did you quack? Perhaps it was because I asked you to, and you decided that obeying those suggestions was in your best interest since you want to improve your life.

Either way, I took you through this experiment to demonstrate how:

*Hypnosis will not make you do anything
you find objectionable.*

You may or may not feel any differently when you are hypnotized than you feel now. During your sessions, you will only accept and perform the suggestions you want. Any suggestion you feel is stupid, immoral, or unwise your subconscious mind will automatically discard.

Can I Really Be Hypnotized?

Here is a short answer: Yes, almost everybody can. If you possess the ability to concentrate for short periods, you can be hypnotized.

In fact, you have probably experienced that experience many times throughout your life. Ever been "spaced out" after being on the computer for a long time? You have experienced a type of hypnosis. Ever suspended your critical mind as you watched an exciting movie or read a good novel? You have experienced hypnosis. Any activity that deeply engrosses you to the exclusion of everything else can become hypnotic. Almost all us have experienced hypnosis in one form or another. (The exceptions are people who have great difficulty concentrating because of medical reasons.)

Professional hypnotists create this feeling on purpose to access your inner mind. That way, you are better able to absorb life-enhancing and specific therapeutic suggestions.

The key to effective hypnosis is to decide it is something you want to do on purpose before each session.

> *Hypnosis is not something you must try hard to do. It is something you agree to allow.*

The state of heightened suggestibility and critical bypass occurs by following a simple procedure that takes you there. It is like following a cooking recipe. If you want to make cookies, you must do what the cookbook tells you. You must collect and add the ingredients with exactness, do the steps diligently, and by the end you could expect excellent cookies. If you questioned the recipe, or failed to follow it or eve changed it, your cookies might not turn out as planned. In fact, they might not even resemble cookies at all!

Hypnosis works when you follow certain precise mechanics. However, if you question it or choose to do things your own way because you think you know better you may not get the best results. Ask yourself these questions first:

* "Do I want to be hypnotized?"

* "Have all my fears about being hypnotized been completely dissolved?"

* "Am I willing to follow easy directions without adding or discarding anything?"

If the answer is "Yes" to all three, then you can be hypnotized on purpose when you are ready. It is up to you.

> *The only real blocks to improving your life with hypnosis are your fears or unwillingness to follow proper hypnotic procedure.*

The Usual Recipe for Hypnosis

There are several simple steps to become formally hypnotized:

Step #1: Relaxation. Most hypnosis sessions begin with some sort of relaxation exercise to release the body from surface tension. The most common technique is "progressive relaxation" in which you concentrate and relax the body one muscle group at a time until the entire body is calmed. All by itself it tends to induce a light hypnotic state known as a "hypnoidal" condition.

There are two types of progressive relaxation: passive and active. The passive kind requires only a mental command for each body part to relax. Active relaxation, on the other hand, works by having you tense and then relax each body part—one part at a time.

**Experiment—
"Active Progressive Relaxation"**

You may do this experiment with your eyes open, though you might have to look away from this page at a certain point:

"Start by placing your attention on your feet and tense all those muscles for the count of three: One ... two ... three.

"Now relax all the muscles of your feet completely. Place your awareness on your lower leg muscles (the calves). To the best of your ability, contract the calf muscles for the count of three: one ... two ... three. Relax them thoroughly before moving on to your upper legs.

"When you are ready, strongly tense the upper legs for the slow count of three: one ... two ... three.

Utterly relax your upper legs. Notice how good it feels to relax your legs and feet

"Concentrate on your buttocks. Right where you are sitting, tighten the button firmly for the count: one... two ... three. Then release all the stress from the buttocks."

This experiment will only work when you willingly use your full concentration and allow your imagination to come forth:

"Pretend there is a magical staircase. And as you descend it makes your mind feel utterly relaxed and free. There are five stair steps in all. Each step causes you to feel twice as deeply relaxed as the step before. Now imagine going down the stairs.

"One... the first step. Use your imagination and allow yourself to feel very relaxed, physically, and mentally. Two... you descend another step. This time you relax mentally twice as deeply, as your mind starts to feel heavier and very tired. Three... twice as deeply as you take the third step. Pretend your mind is slowing down and clearing away all thoughts except for this experience. Four... twice as mentally relaxed as the third step. Pretend your mind is utterly calm and in a state of bliss and serenity. Five... you take the last step now, and step into a deep condition of mental relaxation in which you are completely open to positive suggestion to change your life."

Step #2: The Induction. After physical relaxation, a common hypnotic procedure takes place to relax the critical mental processes called the induction.

There are dozens of possible induction methods. Most of them distract the conscious mind so the subconscious can absorb the coming suggestions unhindered. Many inductions include a number counting procedure, because the numbers subjectively measure the degree of relaxation and the level of hypnosis. The participant's willingness and expectation play vital roles for an induction to be effective.

Experiment—
"Sample Induction"

This experiment will only work when you willingly use your full concentration and allow your imagination to come forth:

"Pretend there is a magical staircase. And as you descend it makes your mind feel utterly relaxed and free. There are five stair steps in all. Each step causes you to feel twice as deeply relaxed as the step before. Now imagine going down the stairs.

"One... the first step. Use your imagination and allow yourself to feel very relaxed, physically, and mentally. Two... you descend another step. This time you relax mentally twice as deeply, as your mind starts to feel heavier and very tired. Three... twice as deeply as you take the third step. Pretend your mind is slowing down and clearing away all thoughts except for this experience. Four... twice as mentally relaxed as the third step. Pretend your mind is utterly calm and in a state of bliss and serenity.

Five... you take the last step now, and step into a deep condition of mental relaxation where you are completely open to positive suggestion to change your life."

Step #3: Hypnotic and Post-Hypnotic Suggestions. Once a satisfactory level of hypnosis happens, the person is ready to accept suggestions from the hypnotherapist.

Sometimes, the first suggestions offered are to encourage deeper relaxation. It could be a simple statement like, "You are going deeper into hypnosis now." Or it could be a more elaborate or image-based suggestion. At other times, various suggestions test the person's hypnosis compliance.

When the desired level of hypnosis has been achieved, suggestions for immediate or future change are offered verbally with something like: "You are now and shall remain a non-smoker." There might also be post-hypnotic suggestions triggered such as "Whenever you see a cigarette you will find the look and smell of it repugnant."

In a single hypnosis session, many types of suggestions may be supplied, but they all center on a single goal such as smoking cessation, weight loss or achieving confidence.

Experiment—
"Hypnotic Suggestion"

Pretend you have successfully entered yourself into hypnosis and you wish to tell your subconscious how successful you will be
with More Instant Self Hypnosis.

Now, say aloud in a quiet and sincere tone, "I am very successful with eyes-open hypnosis, and I succeed with any script I use to reach my goals."

After you say that, think to yourself, "That is a fantastic suggestion and I know it will work for me!"

Step #4: Emerging from Hypnosis. Finally, the person is emerged or "awakened" from hypnosis. This is not the same thing as rousing from sleep. It is simply a return from the hypnotic condition to an everyday state. There is no danger of not being able to emerge from hypnosis. You can emerge from hypnosis whenever you wish.

Experiment—
"Emerging from Hypnosis"

Pretend you have been hypnotized, and the suggestions have been given. Now you are ready to emerge from hypnosis with this sentence: "With your eyes open or closed, count from one to five and tell yourself when you reach the number five that you will return to an everyday state of mind, feeling refreshed and alert."

Again, use your imagination to make this happen.

Self-Hypnosis for Personal Improvement

To the uniformed, the idea of self-hypnosis sounds ridiculous. There was a time, before I started in this career, when I did not realize self-hypnosis was anything more than simple self-talk.

Here is a story about how my mind was changed:

True Story—
"I Discover How Real Self-hypnosis Is!"

One day I was experimenting with traditional self-hypnosis, which took place silently with my eyes closed. I began with progressive relaxation, followed by a simple induction and then I gave myself suggestions to go deeper and deeper.

The problem I often encountered was I became so relaxed I would either fall asleep or lose track of what I was doing.

This time I managed to stay awake and alert and I felt very relaxed, even though I was not certain I was hypnotized.

I wondered what might happen if I gave myself a suggestion that my nose felt itchy. Can you guess what happened next? My nose began to itch intensely!

I was not worried because I knew I had to just exert my conscious willpower so my nose would not itch anymore. And it worked.

You do not have to worry that some unwanted idea will take hold. During self-hypnosis, your mind will alert you to any suggestion it finds questionable. If a suggestion disagrees with you during hypnosis, you simply and silently say "No"—and any effect disappears.

I am glad I had that "itching" experience, because it strongly demonstrated to me how self-hypnosis is as effective as hypnotherapy. After that, I could say with absolute certainty that:

Self-hypnosis is an authentic, achievable method of self-improvement that work on the mind, body, and emotions!

The Importance of Practice and Preparation

The key to success with self-hypnosis is practice and preparation. However, many people quickly get discouraged when they practice it.

With traditional eyes-closed self-hypnosis methods, many people find they often fall asleep, as I did. Traditional methods also require you to prepare and memorize the induction and suggestions ahead of time. This can be a problem for many people because even when you prepare adequately, by the time you have hypnotized yourself the relaxation is so deep it is common to forget the suggestions or even why you chose to hypnotize yourself in the first place! Again, I know this because it has happened to me on numerous occasions. Perhaps it sounds funny; but if it happens to you, it can be frustrating and discouraging.

Luckily, there is a way around these common problems. You will learn about that in the next chapter.

HOW I DISCOVERED THE "EYES-OPEN SELF-HYPNOSIS METHOD"

ONE DAY, I WAS REHEARSING a hypnosis script I had written and planned to record for a client. I was in my home office with the script in my hand and I was walking around as I rehearsed it.

The script included a progressive relaxation, an induction containing relaxing imagery, many therapeutic suggestions, and a common wake-up section to emerge a person from hypnosis.

I immersed myself in preparation as usual. And as I read the script in a quiet and lulling voice, my phone rang suddenly. The sound seemed to pierce my eardrums, a swell of intense irritation, and I felt a strong impulse to smash the phone to bits! In the past, the sound of my phone ringing seemed pleasant.

I stopped my reading, surprised by my overreaction. I knew then I was experiencing a symptom of hypnosis called atmospheric hyperacuity, a term that means that while someone is hypnotized distractions become greatly magnified and disturbing.

As I looked up from my phone, I could feel myself dazed. Everything in the room felt strangely distant and unreal, as if I was a holographic projection.

Because of my hypnosis training and experience, I knew immediately that I was in a strong hypnotic state.

I hypnotized myself with my eyes open while reading the hypnosis script aloud!

As I thought about it for a few moments, it made perfect sense to me. I had been reading in a soothing, lulling tone of voice, and the words I read were hypnotically phrased and full of imagery. Hypnotherapists, too, are not immune to these hypnotic elements and their effects. For instance, I was aware of entering a hypnotic state while hypnotizing my clients.

What was new and startling, though, is that I had hypnotized myself while simply reading a script aloud.

I began to research this phenomenon, but found nothing about it in psychology or hypnosis textbooks or anywhere else. Sure, many books describe the hypnosis and its history, research, and case studies. I already knew that. However, there was no data at all about hypnotizing yourself while reading aloud.

Over the next couple of months, I tried the technique on some of my own challenges like weight control, procrastination and relieving my allergies. In addition, I found that it worked much better for me than traditional self-hypnosis.

It did not take much time to figure out why this new "eyes-open" hypnosis method produces such outstanding results. For one thing, it is virtually impossible to fall asleep while applying it. As I mentioned earlier, it is all too easy to fall asleep while performing traditional self-hypnosis or while listening to a hypnotic audio. However, it is extremely difficult to fall asleep while reading something aloud! Eyes-open hypnosis eliminates that possibility.

Another reason for its superiority over traditional self-hypnosis is that there is no memorization or significant preparation needed. You simply read an induction script, a suggestion script, and a Wake-Up. That's it!

In addition, there is an automatic level of personal involvement required in the "hypnosis as you read" method that is missing in other methods.

For example, although hypnosis audios can be of great benefit, some people tend to be too passive, uninvolved, or inattentive while listening to them. With eyes-open self-hypnosis, constant attention is required to read the scripts. This technique, therefore, tends to produce better results than most hypnosis audios.

Many people have asked me if they can record the scripts from the book and play them back to get the same results. That may work for some people. However, other people might fall asleep or listen to them half-heartedly, and they are the traps we wish to avoid.

If you want the success that so many others have experienced, use the "read aloud" self-hypnosis eyes-open method I talk about. It requires a little more work than listening to a recording, but the effort will pay off with results. Isn't that what you are after: excellent results?

YOUR FIRST SESSION

IN MY BOOK, *INSTANT SELF HYPNOSIS* (called ISH), there is a script designed to induce hypnosis called the Master Induction. The script included here and featured in this chapter contains an improved version of that one called the Master Induction 2.0.

If you are familiar with ISH, you are encouraged to use the newest induction instead of the original. 2.0 can also replace The Reader's Induction from ISH.

Since my first book, I have made many discoveries and innovations based on the experiences of my clients and readers. This new, improved induction is one of those improvements.

Master Induction 2.0 is superior to the 2004 induction in many ways. It is slightly shorter to enable your sessions to take less time to complete. Instead of the imagery of a modern building, 2.0 uses a mansion on a beautiful island which offers a pleasant but powerful and metaphorical message for the subconscious mind. I went to great effort to ensure that every image and phrase would have the maximum hypnotizing effect for all who read of you.

The first time you use the Master Induction 2.0, whether you are new to the hypnosis-as-you-read method or not, read it all by itself. Do not read any other goal suggestion script after reading 2.0.

Read the entire new induction and finish that session by reading The Wake-Up supplied at the end of that induction portion.

That first reading will get you familiar with it. It will condition you to enter self-hypnosis more for your future eyes-open self-hypnosis sessions.

After you do that and after you finish this chapter, you will be ready to put Master Induction 2.0 together with any of the 48 goal suggestion scripts in the next chapter.

For those future sessions, follow the reading of 2.0 by reading the script of your choice. Finish the session by reading The Wake-Up provided at the end of the 48 scripts.

The Eyes-Open Method: How and Why it Works

The Master Induction 2.0 is the induction script that hypnotizes you, as you know. And, when you read it aloud a state of relaxation and heightened suggestibility is established. The Wake-Up section gently and effectively returns you to an everyday state of awareness so you can get on with your day. The entire session (induction, suggestions, and wake-up) takes only about 15-20 minutes.

During your session, you are encouraged to read aloud in a relaxed and soothing tone of voice while imagining you are gently quieting a young child. Your own voice becomes that of a hypnotist that produces a tranquillizing effect on your mind and body.

Many other hypnotic components also contribute to successful hypnosis with this method. The content of 2.0 uses multi-sensory imagery to automatically induce a state of eyes-open self-hypnosis. This is somewhat like what happens when you read a descriptive work of fiction. As you read, your mind cannot help but picture the images presented in the narrative. You may not be aware of this inner visualization process at work, but it is there.

Meanwhile, the conscious mind stays busy by scanning the lines of text to suspend its critical and analytical faculties. In other words, the part of your mind that sometimes blocks positive change is deliberately distracted so that the ideas and suggestions for improvement can go right to the subconscious, the part of your mind that turns those suggestions into realities.

Post-hypnotic suggestions are also included to make your hypnotic experience more effective for subsequent sessions.

In summary, the combination of your own hypnotic voice, the conscious visual scanning of the words on the page and the targeted contents of Master Induction 2.0 predictably produce a condition of self-hypnosis with your eyes open.

You May or May Not "Feel" Hypnotized

It is very important to realize you may not necessarily feel hypnotized during or after eyes-open hypnosis. However, that does not mean you weren't successfully hypnotized.

True Story—
"A Brilliant Friend Says Something Not-So-Brilliant about How the Master Induction Affected Him"

An old high school friend of mine who is now a literature professor at a prestigious American university, wrote to me after he read my first book. He said the induction failed to hypnotize him because he: "...just didn't feel hypnotized."

He had not read the section in the book about how unimportant that is. You do not need to "feel" hypnotized during the session at all.

It seems even college professors are sometimes guilty of skipping important segments of the books they read. By the way, we are still friends today.

The reason you may not "feel" hypnotized is that hypnosis does not necessarily carry with it a feeling. Especially if you are new to this experience, you may not yet recognize when you have successfully entered the hypnotic state. It's important to not expect some strange trance experience. The strange feeling is not your objective anyway. The result is what you want.

You will succeed at hypnotizing yourself with 2.0 the first time you read it if you carefully follow the directions. Then, as you repeatedly use it with your goal scripts, you might feel or notice an unbelievably relaxed state of body and mind, which you might identify as hypnotic. You might even skip words or phrases. You might slur them. You even might add words that are not there. Do not be alarmed when these things occur. They are signs you are simply going deeper into the hypnotic state than during previous readings. Regardless of what you feel or do not feel, remember:

If you are motivated to improve, even lighter states of hypnosis are enough to make the suggestions work.

The real "proof" you have been successfully hypnotized is not with some elusive feeling, but with the positive changes that will occur in your daily life after completing the sessions. You will find it easy, for example, to say no to those extra helpings of fattening foods. You will begin to have a healthy impulse to get to the gym and work out.

That is the real proof that you hypnotized yourself with your eyes open and that this method deliver. Put the technique into operation and trust the process and results rather than looking for some "feeling."

Preparation and Reading Instructions

If you are ready, it is now time to put the Master Induction 2.0 to work. First, here are few simple instructions to make your session successful.

First, find a quiet place to be undisturbed for the required time. Get away from the kids. Put the cat in another room. Tell your partner not to disturb you for the next 20 minutes. Subdue the room's lighting for a calming ambience. However, it should be bright enough to read without strain. Sit in a comfortable chair or sofa.

Have this book with the Master Induction 2.0 narrative in front of you. When you are ready, begin to read it aloud using these guidelines:

* Use a soft, gentle tone of voice, as if you are calming a child.

* Read slowly and pause for a moment wherever you see the ellipses (...).

* Emphasize any italicized words or phrases. It is not necessary to read the words in parentheses ( ) aloud. Just note their content and follow any of their instructions.

* As you read, first relax, and then invest yourself in what you are reading rather (with emotion) than in just parroting the words to yourself.

Important: Make sure to read the entire induction script and suggestion script to the end, including the Wake-Up, in one sitting.

Don't Worry, Don't Think, Just Read!

As some people read the narrative, they might wonder if they are doing it correctly: "Am I using the right voice? Am I visualizing correctly? Am I really achieving hypnosis?" They wonder, analyze, and ponder what is happening so they lose its potential power.

To be successful, suspend your worries and your analytical thinking and just concentrate on reading the script as it is without any self-judgment.

It will work perfectly for you. Tens of thousands of people have succeeded with only minimal effort. Just follow the directions. Do not add to it. Do not subtract from it. Read it as written.

When you read a novel, do you stop after every paragraph and ask yourself: "Am I reading this right? Am I visualizing this scene adequately? Is this book working for me?" No. You do not need to do that. The visualization process while reading a novel is automatic; and no conscious effort is required. It is the same with eyes-open hypnosis sessions. Just read, trust your inner mind to do all the visualizing, immerse yourself in the narrative and have fun with it.

"Master Induction 2.0"

(Begin reading aloud below)

"I hypnotize myself with my eyes open now. I place myself in a comfortable, quiet place where I will not be disturbed, So I can gently and easily concentrate on these words.

"As I feel a sense of privacy and comfort, I use the sound of my voice to soothe my mind and calm my body. I speak slowly ... with a gentle but resonant tone, as if I was reading a bedtime story to a young child I want to feel safe and calm.

"I can feel myself become increasingly relaxed ... as I hear my own voice now ... as though everything is beginning to move in slow motion ... (read slower) slow motion. Moment by moment, my mind becomes as clear as the surface of a calm and quiet mountain lake. Calm ... and quiet.

"And now I picture myself relaxing in a small wooden boat that is gently drifting on a glassy lake. Majestic, tall trees surround the lake. The sun shines and warms my skin. I fully imagine feeling its golden rays on my body, gently soothing and relaxing me from the top of my head down to the tips of my toes (take a few seconds and imagine this).

"As I imagine closing my eyes on the drifting wooden vessel, I hear the leaves of the trees rustling (pause a moment and imagine you hear the rustling) and feel a refreshing breeze pass over my body (take a few seconds to see this) ... and I smell the sweet scent of wildflowers on the wind (imagine the scent of wildflowers).

"I draw a slow breath and release it ... (slowly breathe in and then release it). As I do, I relax twice as deeply and I let go of all stress in my body and mind.... It has been washed away and replaced with an incredible sense of peace and well-being, as I just allow my mind and the boat to move and drift ... carefree ... along the mirror-like surface of the serene water. Just drifting now ... into gentle pathways of peace and solace ... easily ... effortlessly ... the way I might feel on the border of a restful, deep sleep. A restful ... deep ... sleep....

"I imagine opening my eyes to discover the boat has come to a gentle stop upon a lush island. Abundant green plant life looks well-manicured as I notice a trail that leads to a magnificent mansion. As I step out of the boat and slowly walk the trail toward the mansion, the beautiful architecture and grandeur of the great manor mesmerizes me.

"I come to a closed iron gate where a formidable-looking guard is standing and looking at me with a hard glare. However, that glare quickly turns to a smile because the guard recognizes me and opens the gate saying, 'Welcome home.' Relieved, I now realize the mansion and the island belong to me and the guard works for me.

"I walk through the gate and up to a grand, ornate door on which my own first name is embossed in pure gold. As I speak my name aloud (say your first name aloud) the door opens all by itself, as if by some mysterious power. As I step through the threshold of the door, I feel a deep sense of security and well-being. Walking through the vast, beautifully decorated foyer, I see a large portrait of me looking healthy, dignified and successful.

"There are many hallways and rooms to this mansion representing the many aspects of my mind and my life. I make my way to a short stairway with five stairs that lead down to my favorite thinking place in the vast mansion. As I descend the stairs, I count backwards from five to one, and as I do, I use my imagination to relax deeper and to glide into a condition of self-hypnosis, a condition of deep relaxation and heightened receptivity ... with my eyes open.

"Five ... I imagine walking down the stairs and feeling twice as relaxed with each number.

"Four ... the deeper I go the more open to positive change I now become.

"Three ... effortlessly going deeper down the stairs ... feeling safe and secure yet open and receptive.

"Two ... down into a calm and comfortable place ... where creating positive changes is effortless and uncomplicated.

"One ... at the bottom of the stairs now, and I imagine what it might feel like now to be in a state of self-hypnosis with my eyes open.

"I enter into a familiar, welcoming reading room. I approach the most comfortable looking chair and sit down to relax fully. Feeling peaceful and supported, I pick up a book on a table next to the chair. I read the cover with the title, which says: 'Hypnotize Yourself as You Read.' I open the book and begin reading aloud. The words speak to me directly and seem to rise off the pages and into my mind. Here is what they say:

"'You are now hypnotized with your eyes open. Your mind is receptive and suggestible in this state. Every time you read this induction, you automatically go deeper into hypnosis than the time before. You will remain in this deep condition while you read the suggestions. Your mind absorbs the suggestions the way a sponge soaks in water. You easily stay hypnotized with your eyes open until you finish reading the Wake-Up.'"

(If this is your first session, read the following narrative called "The Wake-Up". Otherwise, continue by reading your goal script for your full self-hypnosis session.)

(The Wake-Up)

"I awaken myself from hypnosis safely and easily by counting to five. When I reach the number five I will become fully alert and wide awake. One ... beginning to awaken from hypnosis now. Two ... becoming completely aware of my surroundings as I sense myself awakening. Three ... looking forward with detached expectation to the results from this self-hypnosis session. Four ... I feel wonderful, hopeful, and happy. FIVE ... FIVE ... FIVE ... now wide awake and fully alert!"

Was I Really Hypnotized with Master Induction 2.0?

How did you experience 2.0? Regardless of any feeling or absence of feeling, if you followed these instructions you likely hypnotized yourself successfully.

What Do I Do Now?

Now that you have read 2.0, your mind has been conditioned to enter deeper levels of suggestibility each time you read it. You will be reading it again in conjunction with each of the self-improvement scripts coming up.

You are now ready to move on to the next chapter entitled Forty-Eight Hypnosis Scripts.

48 HYPNOSIS SCRIPTS

In the previous chapter, you used the Master Induction 2.0 to enter hypnosis and condition your mind to the eyes-open hypnosis method. Now, it is time to use 2.0 with the self-improvement suggestion script of your choice.

Perhaps you have already scanned the script titles and you are excited to employ several at a time. Instead, start with only one goal script that is most appealing and inspirational to you. Then follow these easy steps:

* Choose only one script for each session and bookmark it before you begin.

* Find a quiet place where you will not be disturbed for about 20 minutes.

* Subdue the room lighting allowing enough light to read without eyestrain.

* Begin your session by reading Master Induction 2.0 aloud, using a calm and soothing, yet involved tone of voice.

* Read slowly. More slowly when you see "..."

* Emphasize any italicized words or phrases.

* Do not read aloud words found in parentheses. Just take note of their content and follow their instructions.

* After you read Master Induction 2.0, do not immediately read the "Wake-Up" portion. Instead, follow the prompt in parentheses instructing you to turn to the suggestion script you have selected. To do that, turn to the script you have bookmarked and continue to read aloud all the suggestions in that goal script.

* After you have read all the suggestions in the script, read the Wake-Up included at the end of the script. It will safely help you emerge from the hypnotic state. That ends your session.

If there are two script topics that interest you, conduct separate sessions for each goal. For example, you could conduct a session in the morning for the "Joy of Living", then a session in the evening for "Become More Attractive".

I recommend, initially, that you refrain from working on two areas of self-improvement at a time though. Work with one goal at a time for best results. For you all-or-nothing, super exuberant T-personality, risk-taker types out there, here is a short explanation: Your inner mind works best when it is not overwhelmed.

Once you have achieved success with an area of self-improvement, you may then move on to other goals and scripts.

Adopt a "Yes" Attitude

Once you have selected a script for your self-improvement goal, it can be helpful to read the script before starting your first session with it. Beneath each title, you will find a brief description of the issue it addresses. Make sure the script truly pertains to your goal. And to prevent any misinterpretation of the topic, ask yourself these questions before you read further here: "Does it match my goal?" and "Does this resonate and inspire my circumstances and intentions?"

In addition, to promote excellent results from the suggestions in a script it is wise to adopt a "yes" attitude when you read the scripts that apply to you. As you read them, affirm the intention that you will embrace the suggestions. And, have this attitude:

> *"Yes! These are fantastic suggestions and*
> *I KNOW they will work for me!"*

Here is why the "yes" attitude is important. If you are indifferent, uncomfortable, or only hope the suggestions will work for you, your subconscious will take that as an indicator that you believe you will fail, even though you successfully hypnotized yourself.

Again, though you may have hypnotized yourself the suggestions might not work because you did not bring the correction positive intention to the session. Choose to adopt a positive, determined outlook and your subconscious will obey your expectation of successful results.

Although the goal scripts address a broad range of personality types, there may still be the occasional script suggestion that does not fit your personality or circumstances. Do not be concerned. Your mind will automatically discard the suggestion and prevent it from producing any unwanted effects. Even while hypnotized, your mind recognizes undesirable or inapplicable suggestions and rejects them with ease.

Are You Motivated?

You must remember that hypnosis will not make you want to do anything you do not want to do. It just makes what you want easier to achieve. You must truly want what you say you want if you expect hypnosis to help you achieve it.

Honest motivation for your goal is essential to getting positive results. Here are some questions you should take the time to answer:

* Why do I want this change?

* How will it affect me?

* What will I become, have, or do?

* What is the primary emotion I will feel upon accomplishing my goal?

* Am I doing this for myself or for someone else?

* Is my motivation to change stronger than my rationalizations for staying the same (or "stuck in the wrong pattern")?

To increase your chances for success, answer those five questions before the session with the corresponding goal script.

Repeating Your Sessions

You might reach your goal results after the very first session. It happens for many people.

**True Story—
"An Amazing Story About a Man Who Quit Smoking in ONE SESSION!"**

I got an email from a man who said he was so desperate to quit smoking he locked himself in his bathroom to read my Instant Self Hypnosis paperback. He told me that after about two hours—and after using the eyes-open method with the "Stop Smoking" script in the book—he never again smoked another cigarette! He also told me how two years had passed, and how he hasn't even thought about having another cigarette since.

Nevertheless, many readers require more than one session to achieve a complete success. Often, those people should repeat their goal sessions once or twice a day for three to seven days. A few resistant people might need to repeat them for once a day for up to twelve consecutive days. Some might need 21 consecutive. But wouldn't you agree that 21 days is not a long time to overcome a major issue?

How to Fail with the Eyes-Open Method

A small percentage of users of the eyes-open method might fail to get results. Here are the most common reasons why those people fail and how they might improve their chances for success:

> *They believe they were not hypnotized while reading, and they quickly conclude it did not work.* Do not expect to "feel" hypnotized when using these scripts. Follow directions and look for positive changes that will give you enough proof.

> *They are afraid of self-hypnosis.* Dispel those common fears about being hypnotized by reading Chapter 2.

> *They fail to follow the directions to read the scripts properly.* The directions for reading Master Induction 2.0 and getting the most from the 48 suggestion scripts are very important, and they are in Chapters 4 and 5. Please do not skip them.

> *Some people use a script once or twice for their goal, but when they do not get immediate results they stop.* To get results, you might need to repeat your session once a day for three to twelve days consecutively (or even 21 days). If you do not get results after one or two sessions, you are perhaps expecting too much too soon. Remember that for many people the positive results often sneak up on them after several applications. Be patient, stay on task and do the

sessions consecutively until you see results. If you miss a session, just continue where you left off.

They really had not thought about their motivations and inspirations for wanting or needing to change before they started their self-hypnosis session. Take a few minutes and get in touch with the core emotion you think you will feel when you have reached your goal. Be honest. Make sure to be passionate and feel your goal strongly before your session because you must clearly align your motivations to get the results you want.

Ready, Set, Read!

If you have read all the instructions and followed the directions, it is time to perform a session using the script of your choice.

While looking at the scripts, you will notice there are asterisks (*) after some of the hypnotic suggestion sentences or phrases. This is an advanced concept that relates to Bonus #1 near the end of this book. If you are new to the method, please disregard this advanced technique for now. You may apply the advanced technique once you get more experience with the method.

Now, let us move on to the scripts...

BODY, HEALTH & SEXUALITY SCRIPTS

"Become More Attractive"

This goal script encourages the subconscious mind to make inner and outer changes to become more attractive.

"I want to become more attractive, both on the inside and on the outside. *

"With every passing day, I become increasingly attractive to myself and other people as I look in the mirror. There is both an inner and outer change taking place anyone can see as I become more good-looking now. *

"I carry myself like someone who is very attractive. My posture is good. My walk is confident. My voice is clear and sure. Even my facial features change now to reveal a more eye-catching me. It shows in my face. It shows in my body. I am more attractive to others, to women and men. I appeal to both genders and I become increasingly aware of the increased attractive quality I display.

"My body is changing to make me even more attractive day by day. * My subconscious understands what to do to create a more good-looking appearance and I allow myself to enjoy the attention it brings. I want others to find me attractive and show me more attention for my appearance. I go out in public more often. I enjoy going out in public places so others can enjoy how I appear.

"I enjoy looking at myself in the mirror. * When I look in the mirror, I notice most what is attractive about my face and body. I notice how appealing I have become and how I seem to get more so each day. It is now fun to look at myself in the mirror to see the wonderful physical changes as they occur.

"I am more attractive. * I become more attractive day by day. * With each passing day, my appearance improves increasingly. * I look forward to the changes as they continue to happen. I notice that my features are becoming more aesthetically pleasing to me.

"Right now, I imagine what it feels like to be completely at ease and yet to delight in my own physical presence. I imagine looking in the mirror and smiling with joy and satisfaction, because I like the image of myself. I love myself and I appreciate that this beauty has become manifested in my outer appearance. * I imagine others can see my radiant beauty too. As I walk in a public place, I carry myself as an attractive person."

(The Wake-Up)

"I will emerge gently and easily from hypnosis now by counting from one to five. With each number, I emerge twenty percent. When I reach the number five, I will return to everyday awareness.

"One . . . emerging twenty percent, beginning to awaken from hypnosis now. (Speak a little louder and stronger.)

"Two . . . forty percent now, as I become fully aware of my body and environment. (Speak louder and stronger.)

"Three . . . sixty percent . . . I look forward to the positive results from this hypnosis session. (Speak louder and stronger.)

"Four . . . eighty percent, emerging peaceful and happy. (Strongly assert your intention to emerge.)

"FIVE . . . FIVE . . . FIVE . . . One hundred percent now! Wide awake and fully alert!!!"

"Curvy, Slim Body"

This script encourages a healthy, more attractive, and slim feminine body image.

"I feel more beautiful now as I cultivate a slender, curvy, feminine self-image. *

"I now cultivate a positive feminine body look. I picture my body as more slender, curvy, and feminine. * I picture myself as healthy, fit, and beautiful.

"And I recognize all the wonderful benefits that come with having such a lovely body. I will feel lighter and more graceful. I will move and behave more elegantly. I will feel more beautiful on the inside and outside.

"Other people, both women and men, will see me as a woman who has great self-respect, because of the way I take care of my body. They will see me as feminine, fit, and attractive. And that is the image I cultivate for myself right now.

"I take a moment to feel that sense of beauty and femininity that this new body image allows (take 15 seconds to contemplate this).

"It is this beautiful, slim and curvy feminine self-image that now motivates me to do whatever I must to make it a complete and present reality. I know that my mind controls my appetites; therefore, I select the healthiest foods to feel the satisfaction of enjoying my fit, slender, and lovely body.

"I discover that I get more satisfaction from eating smaller amounts of healthy, lean foods that assist me now to achieve my fit body. My appetite changes and regulates itself to desire the correct amounts of nutritious foods, in just the right proportions, to match the curvy, slender self-image I now cultivate.

"My motivation to exercise and be active doubles to accommodate this strong drive to match my slender, feminine self-image. Every time I engage in exercise or sporting activities, I feel a great surge of self-pride and growing satisfaction knowing that I am living up to this beautiful image of myself.

"As I exercise, my body will automatically regulate itself to change into the fit and slender self-image I now cultivate.

"I soon imagine stepping out of the shower and seeing my body in the mirror. I feel a wave of feminine grace, confidence, and pure satisfaction as I see how lean, slender, and lovely I am! I look feminine, sexy, and healthy. This is the way I look and feel all the time now—in or out of clothes.

"It is a great feeling. As I gaze at my fit and feminine image, I think back to when I first started cultivating this image of myself. I marvel that it was easy to change my eating and exercise habits to bring this image of myself into the reality I now experience. I recognize that I am motivated to maintain this lean and potent image of myself.

"I am comfortable with the idea of having a slender, curvy and attractive body image. I am comfortable knowing that I will feel more self-respect and pride. I am comfortable that others, too—men and women—will find me more beautiful and attractive.

"I look forward to having the confidence and poise that come with this body image. And whenever I want to feel a surge of strong female motivation to make this body image real, I run my hand through my hair and say silently or aloud, 'slender and beautiful' three times in a row. And as I do that, the motivating feelings of self-respect and beauty will flow through me ... motivating me to eat the right foods and enjoy more exercise ... to help me achieve a slender, fit and beautiful body."

(The Wake-Up)

"I will emerge gently and easily from hypnosis now by counting from one to five. With each number, I emerge twenty percent. When I reach the number five, I will return to everyday awareness.

"One . . . emerging twenty percent, beginning to awaken from hypnosis now. (Speak a little louder and stronger.)

"Two . . . forty percent now, as I become fully aware of my body and environment. (Speak louder and stronger.)

"Three . . . sixty percent . . . I look forward to the positive results from this hypnosis session. (Speak louder and stronger.)

"Four . . . eighty percent, emerging peaceful and happy. (Strongly assert your intention to emerge.)

"FIVE . . . FIVE . . . FIVE . . . One hundred percent now! Wide awake and fully alert!!!"

"Easy Weight Release"

This script easily encourages healthy weight loss.

"I am ready to easily release excess weight from my body. *

"It is time for me to experience more happiness and enjoy the many benefits of a lighter, healthier and more attractive body. I allow nothing and no one to stand in my way of releasing excess body fat and weight. The decision has been made right here ... right now ... to let go of all that contributes to excess fat and poundage. I dissolve all excuses and rationalizations. I take responsibility and control. That feels very good.

"I imagine myself 65 pounds heavier than I am now. I think about how it feels to lumber around ... how bloated I feel. I feel restricted and encased in excess fat and water. I sweat profusely, feeling uncomfortable, unhappy, and ashamed. It is a very undesirable way to feel and live.

"But now I imagine what it feels like when I have already released all the excess weight. * I am slimmer, trimmer and feel marvelous about the way I look and move. I picture stepping out of the shower and looking at myself in the mirror. I look good and I feel a sense of confidence and poise. I run my hands over my now flat stomach. All the pounds and inches have come off in just the right places. As I step onto the scale, a feeling of utter satisfaction and elation come over me as I see the number on the scale. It is just the right weight for me. This is the way I want to always feel about my body and about myself.

"And I ask myself if I would ever trade these wonderful feelings of health, attractiveness, and confidence for the fattening, sugary or greasy foods: No way! I would not trade the marvelous feelings that come with being slimmer, trimmer, healthier and happier for any food in the world.

"Now I imagine myself in my favorite clothing store trying on a new pair of pants. I discover I must try a size smaller to fit my smaller waist size—and that makes me feel terrific! The smaller size fits me well, and I look good as I look at myself in a three-way mirror—one that shows all the views of my new excellent look. This is a good day! I know I would never trade these feelings for excessive portions of food. No way!

"I can picture myself at a party after releasing all the excess weight. There are buffet tables filled with all sorts of foods I can see and smell. Some of them are healthy and some of them are fattening. As I look over the foods, an acquaintance I have not seen in months barely recognizes me and then gushes about how wonderful I look and how I almost seem like an entirely different person.

"I realize that I am an entirely different person. * I am now a healthy, fit, and more attractive person. As I remember this, it becomes an easy matter to place only healthy foods on my plate, in modest amounts. As I eat these health-giving choices, they taste good and satisfying.

"When the excess pounds drop away week by week, I feel a natural inclination to move my body more. This urge to move may take the form of walking, sporting activities, gardening, doing housework, or anything else that lets me enjoy the improved action and movement of my lighter, leaner body. This increased physical activity makes me feel happy, safe, and comfortable about myself as a physical being.

"When I emerge from this self-hypnosis session in a few moments, I will discover how easy it is to release excess weight. I automatically eat smaller portions of healthy foods that assist me in reaching my goal. I will have no desire for excessive portions of food.

"Every time I say 'No' to an unhealthy food, I am filled with a feeling of empowerment, health and satisfaction."

(The Wake-Up)

"I will emerge gently and easily from hypnosis now by counting from one to five. With each number, I emerge twenty percent. When I reach the number five, I will return to everyday awareness.

"One . . . emerging twenty percent, beginning to awaken from hypnosis now. (Speak a little louder and stronger.)

"Two . . . forty percent now, as I become fully aware of my body and environment. (Speak louder and stronger.)

"Three . . . sixty percent . . . I look forward to the positive results from this hypnosis session. (Speak louder and stronger.)

"Four . . . eighty percent, emerging peaceful and happy. (Strongly assert your intention to emerge.)

"FIVE . . . FIVE . . . FIVE . . . One hundred percent now! Wide awake and fully alert!!!"

"Eliminate Warts"

This script helps the body to get rid of warts.

"I want to eliminate warts from my body. *

"My mind has great power to change and heal my body. Right now, my subconscious mind controls my many body functions. I can communicate with my subconscious through self-hypnosis as I read—to eliminate warts completely from my body.

"My subconscious is my great friend and ally for restoring and maintaining optimum health and appearance. I know my subconscious is willing to accept the suggestion to heal my body of warts, and renew that part of my body with healthy clear skin.

"With my imagination, I can now direct my subconscious mind to heal those useless warts with ease. * I picture how a wart is structured with the many little blood vessels that bring it nourishment. I picture shutting down the capillaries and veins and depriving the warts of nutrients, and they begin to starve. As the warts starve, they now start shrinking. I see those warts shrinking ... shrinking ... smaller and smaller ... until they vanish completely ... to be replaced by new and healthy skin. *

"And now I imagine myself soon. All the warts are long gone. * As I inspect the area where the warts used to be, all I see and feel is healthy, vibrant, smooth skin. I feel a sense of pride and empowerment. I appreciate my mind's ability to heal my body. *

"With this awareness of my ability to create positive change, I instantly become more confident and at ease. I have a positive outlook on my body and my life, and I appreciate myself more than ever."

(The Wake-Up)

"I will emerge gently and easily from hypnosis now by counting from one to five. With each number, I emerge twenty percent. When I reach the number five, I will return to everyday awareness.

"One . . . emerging twenty percent, beginning to awaken from hypnosis now. (Speak a little louder and stronger.)

"Two . . . forty percent now, as I become fully aware of my body and environment. (Speak louder and stronger.)

"Three . . . sixty percent . . . I look forward to the positive results from this hypnosis session. (Speak louder and stronger.)

"Four . . . eighty percent, emerging peaceful and happy. (Strongly assert your intention to emerge.)

"FIVE . . . FIVE . . . FIVE . . . One hundred percent now! Wide awake and fully alert!!!"

"Feel Sexy"

This script will help you recognize yourself as a sexy and sexual person (either gender).

"I feel sexy. *

"I enjoy the idea of feeling and being sexy. When I decide to feel sexy ... I move and behave more playfully and confidently. There is a twinkle in my eyes expressing how I am alive, dynamic, and sensual. Others can notice this spark of sexuality, even when it is subtle. In addition, this is useful not only in sexual situations but also in social and even in business situations. Yes, a deep awareness of myself as sexy can help me in many ways. People are attracted and favor sexy and confident people.

"I increasingly think of myself as a sexy and sexual person. * I recognize my body is a sexual instrument. I take the time to appreciate and love my body in all its sexual and sensual facets. My arms and legs are sexy. My hands are sensual. My chest and back are sexy. My eyes, ears and lips are sensual. My hips are also. Indeed, every part of my body, including my sex organs, is sexy. My body is sensual, and I am a sexual being.

"My sexuality is a fact. I fully embrace my body and my personality as sexy and pleasing. * It brings me great fun and fulfillment to accept this truth about myself!

"Because it is a simple fact that I am a sensual and sexual being, I realize that feeling sexy is a state of mind I can cultivate right away. I choose now to feel sexy and sensual, and to allow myself to enjoy this aspect of life fully. I release any false thinking about sexuality and about myself that have kept me from this enjoyment.

"Instead, I adopt an inner awareness and attitude of sexiness that empowers me. Even now, I can feel that confidence welling up inside me that I can carry with me wherever I go. Because I feel sexy, I can be confident attracting people I want in my life.

"I now imagine being in a social gathering place where I am enjoying the company of someone I find very attractive. I allow my natural sexiness and self-assurance to shine forth. The way I speak and move reveal my inner confidence in my own sensuality. Because I believe in myself, this special person believes in me too.

"In daily social or business situations, I imagine being poised and confident. My sensual qualities express a positive influence over friends and associates.

"And when I am in intimate situations with a partner, I see myself totally enjoying feeling good about being sexual. * There is an ease and a flow to my newfound confidence that increases feelings of intimacy and pleasure. My partner responds very well to my ease and sexual confidence.

"Even when I am alone, like right now, some deep part of me is smiling confidently at my wonderful, unique sexiness and sensuality.

"Being sexy is a natural part of me. * I awaken myself to that and enjoy it. I discover that I am so much sexier than I ever realized. All I had to do was recognize, believe and embrace my sexy self."

(The Wake-Up)

"I will emerge gently and easily from hypnosis now by counting from one to five. With each number, I emerge twenty percent. When I reach the number five, I will return to everyday awareness.

"One . . . emerging twenty percent, beginning to awaken from hypnosis now. (Speak a little louder and stronger.)

"Two . . . forty percent now, as I become fully aware of my body and environment. (Speak louder and stronger.)

"Three . . . sixty percent . . . I look forward to the positive results from this hypnosis session. (Speak louder and stronger.)

"Four . . . eighty percent, emerging peaceful and happy. (Strongly assert your intention to emerge.)

"FIVE . . . FIVE . . . FIVE . . . One hundred percent now! Wide awake and fully alert!!!"

"Feminine Pleasure"

*This script helps women to feel
more pleasure that is sexual.*

"I am ready to enjoy greater sexual pleasure and fulfillment. *

"As I engage in the sexual activity of my choosing, I relax my mind and let my body and subconscious bring forth natural, pleasurable sexual feelings.

"Studies say that sex naturally reduces stress. As I immerse myself in sexual thoughts, feelings, and pleasures—any stressful thoughts about work, home, religion, or childhood memories fade from my mind as mist does before the sun. All that remains is my sexual self, and my desire and attraction for the person of my affections.

"The most important sexual organ is my brain. And my subconscious knows exactly what kind of thoughts, desires and activities tap into the sexual pleasure center in my brain effortlessly and automatically. * Sexual desire and powerful sexual imagery flow freely through my mind and body, arousing me more.

"The touch and even the anticipation of the touch of my partner triggers a feminine sexual response in me to become sexual and intimate. And this sexual response is automatic. My body becomes flushed with sexual desire. I really like that sensation. All I need to do is relax, feel it rise in me and enjoy my sexual pleasure.

"Part of enjoying sexual pleasure is in appreciating my own feminine body and all its functions. I recognize every part of my body as part of my sexual apparatus. My body is beautiful, sexy, and feminine. And I can touch myself during times I want to be sexual and feel how sexy and sexual I am to myself and any sexual partner I may have.

"All my senses become heightened as I playfully encounter my partner's body and touch. My attraction toward my partner is like a sexual current—electric and magnetic. I let this electromagnetic feeling sweep through my mind, emotions, and body, taking me deeper into pure sexual bliss.

"Erotic activity may be simple or creative. Whether it is simple or creative, I enjoy each erotic activity the way one would enjoy a feast of many kinds of wonderful food. Just as I can linger and savor a piece of ripe fruit or a sumptuous gourmet entree, I allow myself to sample and savor the sexual activities I enjoy.

"Sexual pleasure and desire come in waves. * I naturally sense these waves as they rise and fall within me. As I ride the waves of love and erotic pleasure, the peaks of pleasure of these waves grow higher and stronger until my body naturally reaches its erotic peak. As I breathe deeply, I release and let ultimate pleasure run through my entire body. * I have a right to experience this wonderful human pleasure, and I fully and joyously embrace my ecstasy.

"And when the intimate sexual connection finally calms, I feel a profound satisfaction in my mind and body. There is a certainty that I have met my desire and need for sexual contact and intimacy with another human being. I feel proud that I let myself enjoy sex thoroughly and unreservedly.

"It feels good being a sexually satisfied woman. *"

(The Wake-Up)

The Manifestation Revelation

"I will emerge gently and easily from hypnosis now by counting from one to five. With each number, I emerge twenty percent. When I reach the number five, I will return to everyday awareness.

"One . . . emerging twenty percent, beginning to awaken from hypnosis now. (Speak a little louder and stronger.)

"Two . . . forty percent now, as I become fully aware of my body and environment. (Speak louder and stronger.)

"Three . . . sixty percent . . . I look forward to the positive results from this hypnosis session. (Speak louder and stronger.)

"Four . . . eighty percent, emerging peaceful and happy. (Strongly assert your intention to emerge.)

"FIVE . . . FIVE . . . FIVE . . . One hundred percent now! Wide awake and fully alert!!!"

"Firmer, Lasting Erections"

This script encourages firmer and longer lasting erections for men during sexual pleasure.

"I want to experience and enjoy firmer and long-lasting erections during sexual activity. *

"My subconscious completely regulates my sexual functions, including the quality and longevity of my erections. I easily direct myself through hypnotic suggestion to generate firm and lasting erections whenever I engage in sexual experiences. *

"Sexual arousal is natural and automatic. * It is nothing I must work at or try to do. As I relax and allow those instincts to emerge from my deep mind and affect my body, my erections automatically become fuller, firmer, and longer lasting.

"I am relaxed and at ease right now. I let all stressful thoughts about work and social demands drift farther and farther away ... Those things seem distant or unimportant while I enjoy this wonderful hypnotic relaxation. This is a time I have set aside for myself, and I can just let go and enjoy the pleasure of relaxing.

"And I also enjoy the pleasure of letting go when I get sexually aroused. Everything else seems to drift away as I enjoy my growing desire and the way my body automatically responds and becomes excited. As I mentally relax and just enjoy my sexual pleasure, my penis automatically becomes firmer, more erect, and stays that way as I continue to enjoy myself.

"Even allowing my imagination to think freely about sexual situations, positions, and activities, is enough to generate a firm and lasting erection. As I relax, there are certain sexual ideas and images that strongly stimulate my sexual desire and result in a firm, potent erection. *

"When I see and touch my partner, and when my partner sees and touches me, the intensity of my sexual instincts increases my sexually arousal. My desire to feel and give pleasure grows stronger. And as my desire for sexual pleasure rises, my penis becomes very firm. *

"I imagine right now that I am with my partner as we are beginning to be sexually intimate. As each bit of clothing is removed, all non-sexual thoughts and self-consciousness is removed. What remains is my love and attraction for my partner and my growing and strong desire for sexual pleasure.

"It is as though I have entered into a deep sexual kind of trance, where strong and arousing feelings flow easily and freely. I relax and enjoy each sexual moment and let all my senses become engorged with the sensations of sexual pleasure. My penis becomes quickly engorged as well. And I delight in my sexual prowess and the length of my arousal. My penis remains stiff until after I release myself. *

"I will notice how firm my erections become when enjoying sexual arousal. I discover how easy it is to let my mind and body flow instinctively to create strong and long-lasting erections. And I appreciate the confidence this brings me."

(The Wake-Up)

"I will emerge gently and easily from hypnosis now by counting from one to five. With each number, I emerge twenty percent. When I reach the number five, I will return to everyday awareness.

"One . . . emerging twenty percent, beginning to awaken from hypnosis now. (Speak a little louder and stronger.)

"Two . . . forty percent now, as I become fully aware of my body and environment. (Speak louder and stronger.)

"Three . . . sixty percent . . . I look forward to the positive results from this hypnosis session. (Speak louder and stronger.)

"Four . . . eighty percent, emerging peaceful and happy. (Strongly assert your intention to emerge.)

"FIVE . . . FIVE . . . FIVE . . . One hundred percent now! Wide awake and fully alert!!!"

"Go to the Gym"

This script will motivate those who have a gym membership to act and exercise.

"I want to go to the gym regularly. *

"The key to a happy life is balance. And part of that balance is taking care of my body by giving it the right exercise it requires to be fit and healthy. Going to the gym regularly to exercise, I feel more alive, energetic, and balanced.

"Right now, I determine how many times a week I want to go to the gym. I determine at what time I will go. I make a positive commitment to go to the gym at these appointed days and times. I think about the next time I will go to the gym. *

"I joined my local gym because it provides a well-equipped place of enthusiastic people who want to improve the quality of their bodies. There, I can go and focus on the appearance and well-being of my body. *

"I give myself full credit for taking the step to join a gym. This signals to my subconscious that I care about my health and appearance.

"Now it is time to go to the gym regularly and work out my body so I may enjoy the benefits of a fitter, healthier body.

"I imagine myself walking through the door of my gym now. The gym members motivate me greatly. I notice many of them are very fit, healthy, and powerful. Their figures and physiques inspire me. I realize how good it will feel to make the most of my body's fitness potential.

"There are also people in the gym whose bodies are quite out of shape, overweight or weak. Yet I feel inspired by them, because they show the courage and positive commitment to come to the gym and change their bodies.

"As I begin to work out, a strong feeling of enthusiasm fills me. The physical activity makes me feel alive and strong. By just deciding to come to the gym, I am making my whole life better.

"Going to the gym is a treat. * The gym is like a mini-vacation for me. It gives me time to simply focus on my body and my health.

"I picture myself getting ready to go to the gym now. I gather any clothes, shoes, or other items I need to work out properly. I imagine taking the transportation I use to get to the gym. As I get closer and closer, a wonderful sense of balance and satisfaction with my choice emerges.

"As I walk through the door of the gym, I leave the stresses of my life behind. I totally concentrate on my wellness, my fitness, my happiness. * And as I picture myself working out now, I sense the natural stress-reducing hormones filling my body and making me feel extremely happy and alive!

"I am excited about my very next visit to the gym. And I love what going to my gym does for my body, my mind and my whole life."

(The Wake-Up)

"I will emerge gently and easily from hypnosis now by counting from one to five. With each number, I emerge twenty percent. When I reach the number five, I will return to everyday awareness.

"One . . . emerging twenty percent, beginning to awaken from hypnosis now. (Speak a little louder and stronger.)

"Two . . . forty percent now, as I become fully aware of my body and environment. (Speak louder and stronger.)

"Three . . . sixty percent . . . I look forward to the positive results from this hypnosis session. (Speak louder and stronger.)

"Four . . . eighty percent, emerging peaceful and happy. (Strongly assert your intention to emerge.)

"FIVE . . . FIVE . . . FIVE . . . One hundred percent now! Wide awake and fully alert!!!"

"Good Posture"

This script establishes the correct standing and sitting posture to enhance confidence with good body language.

"I display excellent body posture each day. *

"I walk tall, with my head held straight up, my chest out and my shoulders back. *

"My subconscious remains vigilant to keep my posture excellent whether I'm sitting or standing. My posture is like a self-assured, confident, and poised person. *

"My posture as I walk, stand or sit gives me an air of nobility and authority. People can sense this dignity I have. And they respond well to it.

"Right now, even as I am reading this script, I adjust myself in my chair or wherever I am seated. My back is straight yet relaxed. My shoulders are back. My chest is up and out.

"As I adjust my posture, I can feel ... self-confidence come over me. It is as though my improved posture and my feelings about myself are linked. And that feeling of self-confidence is something I want to experience all the time.

"I maintain excellent posture to feel good about myself in all situations. * I hold myself like a royal ... like a king or a queen. Even the regal way I position and move my head displays and supports poise and balance.

"I realize now that the way I position and display my body has a direct influence on the way I feel about myself. Therefore, I choose to have excellent posture always because I enjoy feeling good about myself always. *

"I imagine walking down the street from where I live. Though I walk in a relaxed manner, my head is up and my shoulders are back. And I feel regal, special, good about myself. As people walk by me, they see a person who is confident, self-assured, dignified. They admire the way I carry myself.

"I now imagine sitting at a restaurant. Some of the people around me are slumping in their seats and I feel sorry for them. Because I sit with my back straight and my head upright, when people look at me they see a person with high self-esteem. That is the way I feel, as I sit with good posture.

"I make a habit of maintaining excellent posture. * I recognize that having excellent posture is a secret to having and expressing more confidence. So, anytime I want to boost my self-confidence I check my posture and make it even better. * This improvement in posture makes me feel like royalty. I am poised and I am dignified inside and out."

(The Wake-Up)

"I will emerge gently and easily from hypnosis now by counting from one to five. With each number, I emerge twenty percent. When I reach the number five, I will return to everyday awareness.

"One . . . emerging twenty percent, beginning to awaken from hypnosis now. (Speak a little louder and stronger.)

"Two . . . forty percent now, as I become fully aware of my body and environment. (Speak louder and stronger.)

"Three . . . sixty percent . . . I look forward to the positive results from this hypnosis session. (Speak louder and stronger.)

"Four . . . eighty percent, emerging peaceful and happy. (Strongly assert your intention to emerge.)

"FIVE . . . FIVE . . . FIVE . . . One hundred percent now! Wide awake and fully alert!!!"

"Healthy Choices, Healthy Body"

This script encourages healthy food choices with stress reduction.

"I now become aware of all my lifestyle behaviors. I am determined to make healthy, positive choices. *

"From now on, as I am about to eat a meal or a snack, I become vividly aware of the choices before me ... vividly aware ... of my options with food. And in those vivid windows of awareness and clarity of mind ... I have complete freedom ... to choose the healthiest options for me.

"I can choose to entirely avoid foods that might disrupt my well-being. I can decide which foods will bring me health and happiness. And I will notice ... as I freely choose the healthier foods to eat ... a wonderful sense of satisfaction and great control ... to make the best possible choices.

"I am acutely aware of how I feel through the day ... of how my body feels ... and of my emotional wellness. This heightened awareness gives me the opportunity ... to change how I feel ... and to make better choices. If I discover my body or mind feeling stressed or tense, this allows me the freedom to release those feelings.

"I can easily choose to release stress, tension or negativity by drawing and releasing three slow breaths and saying to myself, silently or aloud ... 'Peace, peace, peace.'* And as I say it, my body and my emotions return to a calm and centered place. * From that place, I can continue to make the best choices for my well-being and the life I want to live.

"Healthy lifestyle choices ... involve simple changes that make me feel better physically and emotionally. I enjoy the freedom of movement ... that comes with making choices ... that grant me greater health and happiness.

"It all begins with my thoughts ... and recognizing how much I care about myself ... and how much I value the freedom of choice ... that good health brings.

"Part of good health ... that gives me the freedom of choice ... is the care I give my body. By choosing to carefully select what I eat ... by giving my body the proper amount of exercise ... and by releasing all unnecessary tension ... I am showing my body the proper amount of love and respect it deserves. In return, my body thanks me ... by maintaining optimum health and performance ... so I can experience greater health and happiness ... every day of my life.

"I imagine now that I am at a buffet table. There are many wonderful looking foods in front of me. As I stand there with my empty plate, I become very aware of my freedom to choose the foods that I want and to avoid the foods that do not serve me well. It is easy to recognize which choices will add to my health and happiness, and I see myself picking those foods, in moderate amounts to put on my plate. As I make the right choices, I feel a wonderful sense of self-respect because I am treating my body and myself well. Now I feel good.

"The buffet table is a metaphor ... for all the areas of life in which I have the freedom to make healthy choices and to feel really good about myself. Because good health means I can continue to have more freedom in every area of life. And that freedom brings the opportunity to experience greater levels of happiness and satisfaction."

(The Wake-Up)

"I will emerge gently and easily from hypnosis now by counting from one to five. With each number, I emerge twenty percent. When I reach the number five, I will return to everyday awareness.

"One . . . emerging twenty percent, beginning to awaken from hypnosis now. (Speak a little louder and stronger.)

"Two . . . forty percent now, as I become fully aware of my body and environment. (Speak louder and stronger.)

"Three . . . sixty percent . . . I look forward to the positive results from this hypnosis session. (Speak louder and stronger.)

"Four . . . eighty percent, emerging peaceful and happy. (Strongly assert your intention to emerge.)

"FIVE . . . FIVE . . . FIVE . . . One hundred percent now! Wide awake and fully alert!!!"

"Increase Metabolism, Burn More Calories"

This script encourages the subconscious to safely increase metabolism and burn more calories.

"I want to safely increase my metabolism to burn more calories and have more energy. *

"My subconscious oversees my body functions, including metabolism. Through self-hypnosis and the power of suggestion, I now instruct my subconscious to begin to safely raise my metabolism to that healthy level most effective for burning more calories and experiencing increased vitality. *

"I will begin breathing deeper on a consistent basis, starting now. Inhale ... (inhale a deep breath) ... and exhale (release the breath fully). As I breathe deeply from now on, the oxygen will increase as well as my metabolism and energy level.

"I will remember how easy it is to take deep, relaxing lung-filling breaths to charge my body and my brain.

"I will also notice an urge to move my body more each day. I find myself stretching my muscles and joints every day. I discover that I walk increasingly, taking the long way so I can enjoy the activity of walking. While I understand and respect the limits of what my body can do, I discover new ways to become more active.

All these activities will assist my body in raising my metabolism ... and burn more calories automatically.

"I imagine now that I am looking at a burning fire in a great fireplace that burns day and night. I select only the best quality wood to place on the fire to make it burn bigger and hotter. I do not put too much wood on the fire at any one time, because that might smother the fire. Instead, I use just the right amount of fuel to enable the fire can thrive. I pick up a bellows and blow more oxygen on the fire and watch it blaze hotter and brighter. And I feel a wonderful sense of satisfaction in tending the fire and making it burn hotter and better.

"The fire represents my metabolism which I want to gently raise. The wood represents food. The bellows represents my level of physical activity.

"My metabolism works day and night to burn calories and fat. And I select moderate amounts of high quality foods to fuel my body at carefully spaced times to encourage my metabolism to raise and burn more calories. I breathe deeply and find ways to move my body to circulate the blood and fill my body with more oxygen ... which increases my calorie-burning and safely raises my metabolism.

"I instruct my subconscious mind to subtly and safely raise my metabolism whenever I eat a meal. * As I sit down during mealtimes and feel the chair beneath me, a post-hypnotic suggestion is activated to safely raise my metabolism to a level that is perfect for burning more body fat and calories. Therefore, whenever I sit down to eat, my subconscious mind will raise my metabolism automatically and safely.

"As my metabolism is raised and burns more calories, my body becomes fitter and my muscles become better toned. And I have more energy and feel more alive than ever before."

(The Wake-Up)

"I will emerge gently and easily from hypnosis now by counting from one to five. With each number, I emerge twenty percent. When I reach the number five, I will return to everyday awareness.

"One . . . emerging twenty percent, beginning to awaken from hypnosis now. (Speak a little louder and stronger.)

"Two . . . forty percent now, as I become fully aware of my body and environment. (Speak louder and stronger.)

"Three . . . sixty percent . . . I look forward to the positive results from this hypnosis session. (Speak louder and stronger.)

"Four . . . eighty percent, emerging peaceful and happy. (Strongly assert your intention to emerge.)

"FIVE . . . FIVE . . . FIVE . . . One hundred percent now! Wide awake and fully alert!!!"

"Love Low Carb Eating"

This script encourages discipline and enjoyment of a low-carbohydrate eating program.

"I love low carbohydrate eating. *

"I choose to now adopt a regular diet of low carb foods and do this with great delight and enthusiasm. * As I decide to release any attachment to sugary and starchy foods, I reap many rewards!

"I love eating low carb because it makes it easy for me to automatically control my weight.

"I love low carb eating because my blood sugar levels remain healthy.

"I delight in only eating low carbohydrate foods because my mood and energy levels remain even, clear and bright! I fully commit to my choice of a low carb eating lifestyle to enjoy becoming more healthy, fit, and happy.

"I dissolve any appetite for the fleeting, disappointing experience of eating high carbohydrate foods. * I realize those foods made me feel sluggish, tired, and irritable. They spiked my blood sugar and made me fatter. I turn my back on those high carb foods and choose now the foods that assist my body in feeling and looking my best. High carb eating made me unhappy and unhealthy. Therefore, I gladly adopt low carb eating as my lifestyle choice because I want to feel happy, healthy, and energetic.

"I love eating low carb because my mood and energy levels are consistent. Even as I think about it now, I feel my mood brighten and balance. * My emotions are no longer being negatively influenced by high carbohydrate foods.

"I imagine standing with an empty plate at a buffet table with a wide variety of available foods. Some are low in carbs, others are high in carbs. There are meats, vegetables, breads, pastas and much more. I automatically find myself bypassing the starchy foods and choosing only low carb foods. It is as though the high carb foods are virtually invisible to me, because they have lost all the appeal they once had.

"It is easy and pleasurable for me to fill my plate only with those low carb foods because they satisfy my taste buds and my appetite completely. As I sit down to eat, I feel a sense of pleasure and satisfaction with my choices even before I eat a single bite. I genuinely enjoy choosing foods low in carbs and passing over high carb foods entirely. And as I eat the delicious low carb foods on my plate, I allow the full taste and texture of the foods to please my palate. *

"I realize that eating low carb is more than a diet for me. Low carb eating is now my normal, everyday way of eating. Some people are vegetarian as a lifestyle and they love it. It is something they choose and they have no desire to deviate from it. Some people are allergic to certain foods. And they avoid foods that cause them harm.

"I love eating low carb foods as a lifestyle. I avoid the high carb foods because they cause my body harm.

"I make eating low carbohydrate foods a wonderful and positive habit. It is now automatic for me to choose to eat low carb. * And as I discover how easy it is to be healthier, fitter, and mentally sharp, I will realize how much I love eating the low carb way every meal, every day."

(The Wake-Up)

The Manifestation Revelation

"I will emerge gently and easily from hypnosis now by counting from one to five. With each number, I emerge twenty percent. When I reach the number five, I will return to everyday awareness.

"One . . . emerging twenty percent, beginning to awaken from hypnosis now. (Speak a little louder and stronger.)

"Two . . . forty percent now, as I become fully aware of my body and environment. (Speak louder and stronger.)

"Three . . . sixty percent . . . I look forward to the positive results from this hypnosis session. (Speak louder and stronger.)

"Four . . . eighty percent, emerging peaceful and happy. (Strongly assert your intention to emerge.)

"FIVE . . . FIVE . . . FIVE . . . One hundred percent now! Wide awake and fully alert!!!"

"Reduce Hot Flashes"

The suggestions in this script assist in the reduction of hot flashes women may experience during menopause or from hormone therapy.

"I reduce the number and severity of hot flashes. *

"My mind is amazing and can now be trained through hypnosis to affect my body. I instruct my subconscious to cool down hot flashes, reducing their severity and frequency. *

"Estrogen has a role to play in regulating my body's temperature. When it fluctuates, my brain sometimes gets the wrong signal and thinks my body is too hot. It tries to cool me off with hot flashes and sweating. But I now can tell my body and brain I'm not overheated through simple imagery and self-hypnosis. And I can control, reduce, and even eliminate hot flashes altogether. *

"I reduce the stress in my mind and body to ease and reduce hot flashes. Stress can sometimes trigger hot flashes; therefore, I do everything to lower my stress levels. Even now, by hypnotizing myself I am dissolving stress because hypnosis naturally relaxes the body and mind. I automatically discover a reduction in the number and severity of hot flashes just by taking this time to hypnotize myself.

"I think of blue as a cooling color now. I can think of a cold icy blue or an airy sky blue or even a comfortable deep and relaxing blue. No matter which blue I think of, just thinking of that color sends a signal to my brain that I feel cool and comfortable.

"I imagine a control knob that looks like the one you might find on the panel of a car's air conditioner. Its knob can be turned to the right toward red to make things warmer, or it can be turned to the left toward blue to make things cooler.

"I can make my body cool and comfortable by imagining turning the knob to the left, toward blue. Whenever I imagine turning that knob toward blue, it signals my brain and my body that my internal temperature is in perfect balance, and there is no need for hot flashes or sweating.

"I can imagine turning that dial even now to reset my body temperature to a much lower level (imagine turning the dial to blue). By doing this, I find a wonderful reduction or even total absence of hot flashes from now on.

"It is remarkable how much control I have over my body. By communicating with it properly, it automatically balances and adjusts my internal temperature to remain comfortable almost all the time. If I find myself beginning to feel too hot, I imagine turning that dial to the left while thinking of blue. And this immediately tells my brain I am not overheating and that I am cool and comfortable."

(The Wake-Up)

"I will emerge gently and easily from hypnosis now by counting from one to five. With each number, I emerge twenty percent. When I reach the number five, I will return to everyday awareness.

"One . . . emerging twenty percent, beginning to awaken from hypnosis now. (Speak a little louder and stronger.)

"Two . . . forty percent now, as I become fully aware of my body and environment. (Speak louder and stronger.)

"Three . . . sixty percent . . . I look forward to the positive results from this hypnosis session. (Speak louder and stronger.)

"Four . . . eighty percent, emerging peaceful and happy. (Strongly assert your intention to emerge.)

"FIVE . . . FIVE . . . FIVE . . . One hundred percent now! Wide awake and fully alert!!!"

"Reduce Stress and Blood Glucose Levels"

This script reduces stress to assist lowering blood glucose (sugar) levels.

"As I reduce my stress levels, I reduce and maintain healthy blood glucose levels.

"I accept the relationship between the mind and the body. I recognize the potential link between stress and blood sugar levels.

"As I now take control over my stress levels through self-hypnosis and the power of suggestion, I experience a positive effect on my blood sugar levels. By eliminating unnecessary stress, I effectively lower my blood sugar to safe and healthy levels. *

"Stress is the body's natural fight or flight mechanism initiated by my brain whenever there is a perceived threat to my well-being. It is a good and life-preserving mechanism if I am ever in danger. However, when there is no danger, there is no need for the stress mechanism to start.

"I now instruct my subconscious mind to allow my body to remain calm and relaxed except in times of physical danger. By remaining calm, I eliminate unwanted stress to allow my other body functions to perform in a balanced and healthy manner.

"I imagine now that there are two big round gauges on a control panel. They are labeled 'Stress Level' and 'Blood Sugar Level.' There is a vibrant green control knob beneath the 'Stress

Level' gauge. I turn the green control knob counterclockwise and I see the meter begin to lower.

"At the same time, I see the meter on the 'Blood Sugar Level' lower at the same time. I realize that whenever I take control to lower my stress level, I automatically safely lower my blood sugar at the same time.

"If I ever feel stressed, overwhelmed, or anxious without an immediate physical threat, I will draw three deep breaths and slowly exhale as I utter silently or aloud: 'Relax, relax, relax.' This signals me to release all unnecessary muscular tension and tightness ... and to feel instantly at ease. As I relax, this signals my body to lower my blood sugar safely and quickly to a healthy level. *

"As I decide to control my stress levels, I also gain more control over my blood sugar levels. I now have an effective means of gaining more mastery over the health of my body. What I desire most is a healthy body with good blood sugar levels."

(The Wake-Up)

"I will emerge gently and easily from hypnosis now by counting from one to five. With each number, I emerge twenty percent. When I reach the number five, I will return to everyday awareness.

"One . . . emerging twenty percent, beginning to awaken from hypnosis now. (Speak a little louder and stronger.)

"Two . . . forty percent now, as I become fully aware of my body and environment. (Speak louder and stronger.)

"Three . . . sixty percent . . . I look forward to the positive results from this hypnosis session. (Speak louder and stronger.)

"Four . . . eighty percent, emerging peaceful and happy. (Strongly assert your intention to emerge.)

"FIVE . . . FIVE . . . FIVE . . . One hundred percent now! Wide awake and fully alert!!!"

"Relieve Chronic Back Pain"

This script is helpful for relieving psychosomatic back pain.

"My back feels healthy, normal and comfortable. *

"My subconscious mind is very powerful. I know that it sometimes creates discomfort in various parts of my body to distract me from strong feelings of rage or sorrow that I have been hiding from myself. My mind sometimes creates pain in my back to keep me from feeling strong emotions it thinks I cannot handle.

"I appreciate that it wants to protect me this way. However, I now decide to discontinue manifesting pain in the body as a distraction from difficult emotions. Therefore, I instruct myself to discontinue creating distractions of pain in my back or any other part of my body.

"I instruct it to return the blood flow and oxygenation in the back to normal. * Return the blood flow and oxygen of those nerve endings to normal, healthy levels. *

"As I read these words, I simultaneously place my awareness on my back where the discomfort lies. I now picture that part of my body able to breathe in and out much the same way I breathe with my lungs. I see it drawing in relaxing breaths of oxygen and releasing all emotional tension (draw two breaths and imagine this).

"Now I picture those breaths are made of a pure golden color ... that the air my back breathes in has a golden yellow hue (draw in two breaths and imagine this). As I release these breaths, I notice that all discomfort releases from my body too. The area I am focusing on returns to feeling normal, healthy, and pain-free. *

"I now imagine that my whole body can breathe in the same way. Every time I draw in a breath through my nose and mouth, I simultaneously imagine my whole body draws in the golden yellow air that soothes and normalizes my whole body and my entire nervous system (draw three slow breaths while seeing this). My body is now free of any psychosomatic discomfort. * And it will remain that way because I have instructed my subconscious to do so."

(The Wake-Up)

"I will emerge gently and easily from hypnosis now by counting from one to five. With each number, I emerge twenty percent. When I reach the number five, I will return to everyday awareness.

"One . . . emerging twenty percent, beginning to awaken from hypnosis now. (Speak a little louder and stronger.)

"Two . . . forty percent now, as I become fully aware of my body and environment. (Speak louder and stronger.)

"Three . . . sixty percent . . . I look forward to the positive results from this hypnosis session. (Speak louder and stronger.)

"Four . . . eighty percent, emerging peaceful and happy. (Strongly assert your intention to emerge.)

"FIVE . . . FIVE . . . FIVE . . . One hundred percent now! Wide awake and fully alert!!!"

"Strong, Lean and Powerful Body"

*The following suggestions promote a
lean and strong male body.*

"I feel great satisfaction when I think of my body being strong, lean and powerful. *

"I now cultivate a positive masculine body image. * I picture my body with lean muscle. * I picture myself as strong, powerful, and fit. * I know all the wonderful benefits that come with such a fine body. I know I will feel confident with this new image of strength and fitness. I will feel healthy on the inside and on the outside.

"With this healthy, strong body, I will carry myself with self-respect and dignity. People will see me as an energetic and healthy man who is vital and capable. I feel truly proud now as my new strong body shows my inner power and motivation. I take a moment now to bask in how makes me feel (wait 15 seconds) ....

"It is this self-image of a powerful, fit and lean body that motivates me to do what I must to bring it into full reality. I know that since the mind controls my appetites, I will select the healthiest foods to feel the satisfaction of possessing a lean, powerful, and fit body.

"I discover that I get more satisfaction from eating smaller amounts of healthy, lean foods that assist me in achieving my fit body. My appetite changes and regulates itself to desire the correct amounts of nutritious foods, in just the right proportions, to match the lean, strong person I am.

"My motivation to be more active doubles now to go with this strong drive which fits my powerful, self-image. * And every time I exercise or enjoy vigorous sporting activities, I feel a great surge of pride and satisfaction. As I exercise, my body will automatically regulate itself to change into this new powerful and fit image. *

"I imagine myself soon. I am stepping out of the shower to see my body in the mirror. I feel a wave of strength, confidence, and pure satisfaction as I see how lean and powerful I am! I look strong, sexy, and vital.

"Now... this is the way I look and feel all the time—in or out of clothes. It is a great feeling. In addition, as I think about my fit and masculine image, I remember when I started developing this. I marvel that it was easy to change my eating and exercise habits to make this new, strong image of myself real.

"And I am excited and motivated to maintain this lean and potent image of myself.

"I am comfortable with the idea of having a lean and commanding body image. I am comfortable knowing that I will feel more self-respect and confidence. I know others will find me more masculine, powerful, and attractive. I look forward to having the confidence and authority that comes with this body.

"Whenever I want to feel a surge of strong motivation to bring this body image to powerful reality, I make a fist and say silently or aloud, 'fit and powerful' three times in a row. *

"When I do, the feelings of self-respect and vitality will surge through me ... cheering me on to eat the right foods and enjoy more exercise ... to help me achieve a lean and powerful body."

(The Wake-Up)

"I will emerge gently and easily from hypnosis now by counting from one to five. With each number, I emerge twenty percent. When I reach the number five, I will return to everyday awareness.

"One . . . emerging twenty percent, beginning to awaken from hypnosis now. (Speak a little louder and stronger.)

"Two . . . forty percent now, as I become fully aware of my body and environment. (Speak louder and stronger.)

"Three . . . sixty percent . . . I look forward to the positive results from this hypnosis session. (Speak louder and stronger.)

"Four . . . eighty percent, emerging peaceful and happy. (Strongly assert your intention to emerge.)

"FIVE . . . FIVE . . . FIVE . . . One hundred percent now! Wide awake and fully alert!!!"

MIND, BEHAVIOR &
SPIRIT SCRIPTS

"Achieve My Potential"

These suggestions motivate you to find and seek your fullest potential.

"I want and I am ready to achieve my potential in life. *

"I can become, attain and acquire more than I have yet to imagine. I refuse to settle for less from life. I refuse to settle for less from myself. It is time to feel motivated and live my life passionately and with excellence.

"I'm capable of much more and I'm willing to do whatever it takes to reach my potential. If I need to learn more, I find ways to become better educated. To obtain new skills, I find those who can teach me. If I need to shake hands to get where I want to go in life, then I find those hands to shake and I network. To reach my physical peak, I alter my eating and exercise habits. Whatever I want to achieve, I set my whole mind and body to act now.

"I recognize that things take time and effort to achieve. I break down my larger goals into smaller ones and fulfill those goals one by one until I achieve my goal.

"I stay positive as I put my goals in motion. I dissolve all negativity, whether it comes from my own mind or from the minds of others. *

"I establish a balance within myself. I am self-disciplined and forgiving if mistakes are made. Mistakes lead me closer and closer to my potential.

"I take full responsibility for what happens in my life. I stop blaming people, society, or institutions for my circumstances. Any unfair treatment from the past or the present only makes me stronger. In addition, the more powerful I get, the more fully I can live my possibilities.

"I build in my imagination a picture of my most successful self. I look healthy, attractive, and secure. I am dressed in fine clothes and have a regal bearing. In my eyes, there is a look of strength, high self-esteem, wisdom, and compassion. I carry the look of success and achievement. *

"The power to change, improve and reach for what I want to be and have and do is mine to create. I now use that power to spring forward in my life and live it to the fullest. I see every circumstance and every person that comes my way as opportunities to learn, live, grow. *

"A powerful shift is taking place in me during this self-hypnosis session. * I will discover from this moment forward that I have a 'Can Do!' attitude about what I want to do. I find that life is worth living on many levels I previously took for granted or that I simply did not notice.

"But now I notice it. I see that life is good and full of opportunities for me to become more successful. With every passing day, I grow increasingly into the picture of my most successful self.

"I live to my fullest potential now."*

(The Wake-Up)

"I will emerge gently and easily from hypnosis now by counting from one to five. With each number, I emerge twenty percent. When I reach the number five, I will return to everyday awareness.

"One . . . emerging twenty percent, beginning to awaken from hypnosis now. (Speak a little louder and stronger.)

"Two . . . forty percent now, as I become fully aware of my body and environment. (Speak louder and stronger.)

"Three . . . sixty percent . . . I look forward to the positive results from this hypnosis session. (Speak louder and stronger.)

"Four . . . eighty percent, emerging peaceful and happy. (Strongly assert your intention to emerge.)

"FIVE . . . FIVE . . . FIVE . . . One hundred percent now! Wide awake and fully alert!!!"

"Assertive, Confident Salesperson"

This script assists the salesperson in becoming more confident and assertive in business situations.

"I want to now become a more assertive, successful salesperson. *

"I am ready to confidently initiate conversation and build rapport with customers and clients to experience the joy of greater success.

"I am a unique individual, which means there is no other salesperson exactly like me. Customers like my unique and friendly personality that I bring to my presentations. Because they like me, they are more likely to purchase what I offer. I am persuasive, knowledgeable, and effective in sales.

"Successful selling depends on the relationship and intelligent conversation between me and my perspective clients. I begin building that relationship with some small talk. Then I look for something we have in common. As I listen to how the customer communicates, I find a way to match their style. If the customer speaks fast, I speak fast. If they speak slowly, I speak slowly.

"I pay attention to the customer and focus on what they say and do with genuine interest. This makes the customer more interested in me. The more we talk, the more the customer trusts me. Sometimes, this will take some time or even more than one conversation. That is fine.

"My job as a salesperson is not to force anyone to do anything. Instead, I offer information and potential solutions they may not realize.

"All interactions I have with a customer, even those not directly dealing with sales, provide me with the opportunities to expand my understanding about the customer's life. The more I understand my customer, the more I understand how my services or products can fit their needs and desires.

"People buy things when it makes sense for them to do so. When the reasons in my offer, proposal or presentation are strong and compelling enough—those people will buy from me!

"Sometimes customers aren't ready to buy after our first conversation. This is completely okay. However, by building a relationship with the customer, they are likely to return to me when they are ready to buy. They will remember my sincerity and professionalism.

"I imagine coming face to face with a perspective client now. This potential customer happens to speak somewhat quickly. I subtly adjust my way of talking to match his quick speaking style. As I ask questions, I look for common ground. When I find similarities, I let the customer know in how we are alike. I can feel the customer beginning to relax and feel a rapport with me. I inform the customer how my service or product meets their needs. At the end of the conversation, I can sense the customer likes what I offer. I ask for the sale. The customer says "Yes".

"I'm an excellent and assertive salesperson. * My confidence in my personality and the way I sell products and services increases daily. * I recognize there is a place in my market for someone like me. I use my personality and powers of observation to become outstanding in sales. I'm excited to bring my unique skills and gifts to perspective clients and customers."

(The Wake-Up)

"I will emerge gently and easily from hypnosis now by counting from one to five. With each number, I emerge twenty percent. When I reach the number five, I will return to everyday awareness.

"One . . . emerging twenty percent, beginning to awaken from hypnosis now. (Speak a little louder and stronger.)

"Two . . . forty percent now, as I become fully aware of my body and environment. (Speak louder and stronger.)

"Three . . . sixty percent . . . I look forward to the positive results from this hypnosis session. (Speak louder and stronger.)

"Four . . . eighty percent, emerging peaceful and happy. (Strongly assert your intention to emerge.)

"FIVE . . . FIVE . . . FIVE . . . One hundred percent now! Wide awake and fully alert!!!"

"Astral Travel Tonight"

*This script encourages an out-of-body experience.
Recommended: Read just before bedtime.*

"I am ready to experience astral travel tonight. *

"After I go to sleep tonight, I will have a self-aware out-of-body experience. * I will experience myself in my astral body and enjoy safely travelling on the inner planes of reality. *

"Having an out-of-body experience is a joyous adventure that may prove to me that I exist beyond the physical dimension. It is a voyage to other dimensions and possibilities.

"Astral travel is a natural phenomenon. People often experience astral travel while sleeping, yet they fail to remember their experiences or else they mistake their journeys for a dream. My mind will alert me when I have left my physical body to become liquid and lucid my out-of-body experiences and remember them.

"I dissolve fears or worries about astral travel. I can return to my physical body at any time by the simplest desire to do so. In the unlikely event that I am not enjoying my out-of-body journey, I return to my physical body safe and secure.

"I'm an astral traveler tonight. *

"I imagine that I have already gone to sleep. I suddenly find my mind active and aware even though my physical body remains asleep. I discover that I am floating near the ceiling of my bedroom, looking down at my physical body several feet below me. I am astounded; I remain calm though, at peace and completely self-aware. I become alert to the fact that I am having an out-of-body experience.

"And I feel a sense of freedom, wonder and joy. I see, hear, feel and experience things while astral travelling. At first, I choose to stay in my own bedroom, and within the rest of my home.

"But then I discover I can go wherever I want to go and even venture to planes of reality I never imagined. Therefore, I enjoy my travels out of the body until I sense it is time to return to my physical body. When I do, I discover I automatically return to my physical body and awaken naturally. When I awaken, I remember my journeys while away from my body. I feel greatly empowered by this ability of mine.

"I relax and expect to experience and remember having an out-of-body experience this very night*. Astral voyages are common and natural. And through suggestion, I now give my subconscious permission to allow me to lucidly experience astral travel to expand my awareness of myself and the universe.

"I astral travel tonight. *"

(The Wake-Up)

"I will emerge gently and easily from hypnosis now by counting from one to five. With each number, I emerge twenty percent. When I reach the number five, I will return to everyday awareness.

"One . . . emerging twenty percent, beginning to awaken from hypnosis now. (Speak a little louder and stronger.)

"Two . . . forty percent now, as I become fully aware of my body and environment. (Speak louder and stronger.)

"Three . . . sixty percent . . . I look forward to the positive results from this hypnosis session. (Speak louder and stronger.)

"Four . . . eighty percent, emerging peaceful and happy. (Strongly assert your intention to emerge.)

"FIVE . . . FIVE . . . FIVE . . . One hundred percent now! Wide awake and fully alert!!!"

"Attract a Mate"

This script assists in building a positive and expectant attitude toward finding a suitable romantic mate.

"I want to enjoy the act of attracting a healthy and loving relationship. *

"I am now ready to attract a healthy romantic relationship, and I allow this awareness to manifest into my life a worthy, loving mate. *

"Because of my decision to attract a loving relationship, events and circumstances will come together to bring me just the right person. This special someone will be very attractive to me physically, mentally, emotionally, and in all other ways that matter to me. This individual will also find me very attractive and compatible in all-important ways.

"I trust the universe and my intuition to bring the right mate to me. I will attract someone on my level of growth, with a well-matched life path. We will quickly recognize all that we have in common and begin a beautiful relationship.

"I expect to find this special someone any day now. I am at total peace as I wait for our first encounter. All doubt and anxiety vanish as mist before the sun as I feel my ideal companion drawing closer to me.

"While I am confident and at total ease, I pay attention to new and familiar people I encounter each day. That special someone may be among them, and I will observe opportunities or unusual coincidences that indicate the possibility of a budding romance for me.

"I imagine, for example, I am attending a party. There are many people at the party, some of whom I have known for a long while. Others I have never met before. With a sense of ease and patience, I notice and observe every person I speak with, whether they are a new acquaintance or an old one. I know who I find attractive. I realize who finds me attractive.

"And now I imagine there is one person I find very appealing. We are talking. There is a lot of eye contact and subtle flirtations that tell me this may be the person I have been searching for.

"I listen to my heart, to my intuition and to my rational mind to know if it is right to be open about pursuing a relationship beyond this.

"Loving companionship is a basic human desire. I have a right to want that. I have a right to attract a loving relationship right now.

"By using hypnosis to attract a mate, I will discover change occurring in myself and in my life. I will radiate a subtle signal to potential lovers leading to the possibility of romance and connection.

"And just as my mate is being drawn to me and my life, I am being drawn to that person and their life as well. Day by day, the universe is assembling circumstances and situations so we will come together romantically.

"I am ready to attract a mate. That amazing person is ready for me too. Our paths will intersect any day now."

(The Wake-Up)

"I will emerge gently and easily from hypnosis now by counting from one to five. With each number, I emerge twenty percent. When I reach the number five, I will return to everyday awareness.

"One . . . emerging twenty percent, beginning to awaken from hypnosis now. (Speak a little louder and stronger.)

"Two . . . forty percent now, as I become fully aware of my body and environment. (Speak louder and stronger.)

"Three . . . sixty percent . . . I look forward to the positive results from this hypnosis session. (Speak louder and stronger.)

"Four . . . eighty percent, emerging peaceful and happy. (Strongly assert your intention to emerge.)

"FIVE . . . FIVE . . . FIVE . . . One hundred percent now! Wide awake and fully alert!!!"

"Attract Surplus Money"

The suggestions of this script will assist in manifesting extra money to help enjoy life more.

"I attract surplus money. *

"While I'm genuinely thankful that all my basic needs have been met, I now use the power of my mind to manifest surplus money to experience more enjoyment from life. *

"I imagine what it feels like to have already manifested extra money to spend however I choose. I picture looking at my checking or savings account statement and feeling so good when I see how much extra money I now have. It feels good to know I can put money toward things that make me happy. I feel secure knowing I have money in savings whenever I need it.

"Now I think about what it is I want to do or have with this surplus money. I picture myself paying for something I really want with the same sort of glee a young child expresses when paying for candy. Pure joy! Now I see myself enjoying what I paid for. In addition, I am thankful that I am experiencing the fulfillment of my desires.

"I graciously permit myself to enjoy surplus money in ways that please me.

"I imagine money falling from the sky as I hold out a strong, open cloth bag to catch it. I see gold and silver coins, precious jewels, paper money and checks made out in my name raining from the heavens. As I reach out with my bag, I imagine my bag's opening growing larger and larger, allowing me to catch the bounty and hold more wealth. I watch as the coins, jewels, and money fall into my sack. It becomes so full it starts spilling over onto the ground below. A great feeling of abundant wealth and satisfaction are mine.

"I open myself to receive overflowing amounts of money and wealth now.

"And now I stand beneath a tree holding a rake. The tree leaves are made of dollar bills and are falling to the ground as if it was a windy day in autumn.

"I rake the money toward me. The leaves of this money keep on frantically falling and covering the ground, and I have great fun forming a great mound of leafy dollars totaling such a huge mound of wealth in the form of $100 bills!

"With complete joy, I jump into the soft pile of money and roll around in it like I'm a child at play. I throw some of it around and into the air and have a lot of fun with my newfound wealth. This extensive treasure pile is just for me and I can do what I want with it.

"I harvest a great surplus of money. *

"New opportunities to manifest surplus wealth and money come my way. I open my mind to receive and accumulate extra wealth. My subconscious uses its untold resources to bring surplus money to me quickly. I look forward to using my extra riches toward things that bring me happiness, pleasure and satisfaction."

(The Wake-Up)

"I will emerge gently and easily from hypnosis now by counting from one to five. With each number, I emerge twenty percent. When I reach the number five, I will return to everyday awareness.

"One . . . emerging twenty percent, beginning to awaken from hypnosis now. (Speak a little louder and stronger.)

"Two . . . forty percent now, as I become fully aware of my body and environment. (Speak louder and stronger.)

"Three . . . sixty percent . . . I look forward to the positive results from this hypnosis session. (Speak louder and stronger.)

"Four . . . eighty percent, emerging peaceful and happy. (Strongly assert your intention to emerge.)

"FIVE . . . FIVE . . . FIVE . . . One hundred percent now! Wide awake and fully alert!!!"

"Become a Leader"

This script encourages taking on leadership.

"I become a leader in life. *

"I step forward and take initiative to lead small or large groups of people, whether socially or professionally. *

"I believe in my intelligence and capabilities and I am confident that I make a fine leader. * While there are times when I can and should follow others in a chain of command, now I take charge of life situations with groups of people.

"I am bold and decisive, and I now choose to use my initiative to become a leader whenever it is warranted. I am full of an energetic desire to lead so I step up to the plate and become the leader that I know I really am.

"My ideas are excellent. Others respond to my ideas and my leadership. They are looking for leaders. There are too many followers in life. I choose to lead. I have a 'can do' attitude. I grow confident in my ability to lead others.

"I imagine being in a group of people, many of whom seem to wander and have no particular direction. I step forward and announce to them that I am willing and able to lead them, to give them direction and purpose. The group is very happy and excited to have my leadership. They want me to lead them. They want me to give them direction and to delegate and deploy. I feel a sense of satisfaction as I see them acknowledge my leadership. I realize now that people are waiting for good leaders.

"I am a good leader. I am a good leader because I know how to lead people with fairness and authority. I balance compassion and authority in all my decisions. And people respond well to that kind of leadership.

"I look forward to opportunities to lead. I enjoy making decisions for groups of people. I enjoy stepping out of the crowd and taking charge of situations and events. It is fun to lead. And I like the way leading makes me feel about myself: that I'm confident, smart, empowered."

(The Wake-Up)

"I will emerge gently and easily from hypnosis now by counting from one to five. With each number, I emerge twenty percent. When I reach the number five, I will return to everyday awareness.

"One . . . emerging twenty percent, beginning to awaken from hypnosis now. (Speak a little louder and stronger.)

"Two . . . forty percent now, as I become fully aware of my body and environment. (Speak louder and stronger.)

"Three . . . sixty percent . . . I look forward to the positive results from this hypnosis session. (Speak louder and stronger.)

"Four . . . eighty percent, emerging peaceful and happy. (Strongly assert your intention to emerge.)

"FIVE . . . FIVE . . . FIVE . . . One hundred percent now! Wide awake and fully alert!!!"

"Better Golf Score"

The following suggestions increase focus and confidence while playing competitive golf to obtain a better score. Note: This script does not teach game mechanics. Some prior golf technique instruction is required.

"I want to improve my golf score. *

"I use self-hypnosis now to automatically focus during the game. * My intense focus will enable me to confidently tap into my golf skills and knowledge. When I easily tap into improving my golfing skills, a better score becomes the natural result. I easily take strokes off my game. *

"I trust the expert instructions I have received about how to play golf. I understand and remember the fundamentals of excellent stroke-making. Already the memory of making good shots is implanted in my mind. I already know what excellent drives, chips, and putts look like and how they make me feel. The knowledge is here inside of me like a computer.

"I now engage completely in the process of practicing excellent golf form and energy, rather than just the final score result. Before I begin playing, I already embrace my intention to have a great score. However, as I begin to play, I let go of the outcome and concentrate on the enjoyable process of playing golf.

"And by letting go of the possible results of the game, I free my mind to totally focus and enjoy the process of excellent shot-making.

"Whenever it is my turn, I let go of everything and everyone else, and simply concentrate on what I'm doing.

"I imagine watching myself from the outside as I prepare and line up a shot. I see myself with 100% focus and confidence getting ready to strike the ball. I imagine a look on my face of calm energy as I get into the flow of the stroke. As the club hits the ball, I see it glide gracefully where I intend it to go exactly.

"From now on, after I have lined up the shot, but right before I strike the ball, I say to myself silently or aloud: "Flow!" And as I say the word—"Flow!"—and begin my stroke, it is as though my mind and body become one with the swing and I feel connected. * With the perfect mixture of calm control and muscular tension, I contact the ball, and I observe a magnificent and accurate shot.

"Whether it is a drive, a pitch, a chip, or a putt, saying the word "Flow" puts me into the perfect flow of connection with this golf game I enjoy. * My swings are balanced and easy as though they were all automatic. *

"I imagine I have just finished the last hole of the game. As I look at my score, I am delighted and amazed my score has lowered. By deciding to focus and enjoy the process of the game, my score improves.

"And every time I play or practice, my mind and body make new improvements I can trust. Therefore, when I play competitively, I can access the greater skill levels, using my magic word 'Flow.' In addition, when I do, I can expect more accurate shots that give me better and better scores. This brings me more joy from golf than ever."

(The Wake-Up)

"I will emerge gently and easily from hypnosis now by counting from one to five. With each number, I emerge twenty percent. When I reach the number five, I will return to everyday awareness.

"One . . . emerging twenty percent, beginning to awaken from hypnosis now. (Speak a little louder and stronger.)

"Two . . . forty percent now, as I become fully aware of my body and environment. (Speak louder and stronger.)

"Three . . . sixty percent . . . I look forward to the positive results from this hypnosis session. (Speak louder and stronger.)

"Four . . . eighty percent, emerging peaceful and happy. (Strongly assert your intention to emerge.)

"FIVE . . . FIVE . . . FIVE . . . One hundred percent now! Wide awake and fully alert!!!"

"Brighten Your Aura"

The following suggestions strengthen and brighten the aura (aka personal magnetic field) to assist in self-protection, more healthiness, and attracting success.

"I strengthen and brighten my aura now. *

"Through the power of suggestion and imagination, I easily charge and brighten my aura. With a bright aura, I can experience greater protection from harm, better mental and emotional healing, and health. And I will discover success flows more easily to and from me.

"As I breathe I imagine the air is made of gold and yellow light. And as I breathe in, I am bringing that golden yellow energy into my body (take a breath and imagine this) ... The golden yellow radiance fills my lungs.

"As I exhale, that radiant light goes to every organ, every cell, every nerve ending and all other parts of my body (exhale and imagine this) ... This radiance particularly fills the center of my chest. It forms a bright sphere of golden yellow ... like a miniature sun. That sun's center shines a powerful aura of light that surrounds my entire body and extends far from me.

"I picture feeling the power of this radiant light giving me strength, vitality and a bright disposition. The light vanquishes any undesirable conditions in my body. The field of surrounding light protects me from negativity. Undesirable things are automatically repelled or dissolve as they approach my aura.

"Every breath I take vitalizes and circulates my bright, protective aura of light. * Now there is an unlimited supply of energy available to me.

"Because my aura is bright and powerful, I automatically attract success and happiness, because like things attract. Whatever is sunny, happy, and healthy is attracted to me, just as I am now automatically attracted to it.

"My aura remains bright and powerful for minutes and hours that follow this session. * Every time I repeat this session my aura brightens faster and more powerfully.

"As I pay attention after this session I become aware of the overt and more subtle ways in which having this bright aura enhances my life."

(The Wake-Up)

"I will emerge gently and easily from hypnosis now by counting from one to five. With each number, I emerge twenty percent. When I reach the number five, I will return to everyday awareness.

"One . . . emerging twenty percent, beginning to awaken from hypnosis now. (Speak a little louder and stronger.)

"Two . . . forty percent now, as I become fully aware of my body and environment. (Speak louder and stronger.)

"Three . . . sixty percent . . . I look forward to the positive results from this hypnosis session. (Speak louder and stronger.)

"Four . . . eighty percent, emerging peaceful and happy. (Strongly assert your intention to emerge.)

"FIVE . . . FIVE . . . FIVE . . . One hundred percent now! Wide awake and fully alert!!!"

"Deeper Voice"

This script will help deepen the register and resonance of the speaking voice to project more authority.

"I want to speak with a deeper, more clear and resonant voice. *

"From now on I speak with a deeper, richer vocal pitch. * Even as I read this hypnotic script aloud, I find a vocal tone and pitch that has a strong, resonant sound. I read this entire script with that voice.

"The power for this voice comes from the diaphragm rather than my throat. I use the diaphragm, just like professional speakers and singers, to produce strong and resonant sound that projects a strong and confident personality.

"I keep the register of my regular speaking voice deeper and more resonant now and forever. * I speak with a rich resonance and pleasant pitch. The sound of my voice is more pleasing and authoritative.

"I use my diaphragm to speak with power, clarity and at a low and resounding pitch. If I ever discover myself speaking in a high or shrill tone, I immediately drop the pitch and recover the rich tone of my natural voice. Because it is now natural and normal for me to speak in a lower register using my diaphragm. (Lower your voice and speak slower now.) This enables me to get more air into my voice so that it carries farther and sounds true, deep, and authoritative.

"I feel more confident as I use my deep and resonant speaking voice. * It is my true voice. The lower pitch of my voice reminds me that I am a poised and confident person who expresses words and opinions that are clear, intelligent, and worth hearing.

"To make sure I have found my true voice, I place my concentration right now on my diaphragm, just below the ribcage. I imagine that my voice is coming from this area of my body. The vocal quality, pitch and tone rise from this area. And I can hear and feel a stronger deeper voice coming forth from my body now. The sound is richer, more powerful, and fuller than before. It is my true voice. I now use my deeper true voice on a regular basis.

"Right now, because I am speaking aloud, I practice using my deep, resonant and natural speaking voice. I find a comfortable pitch and sound as I read these words. It is easy to find this sound, because it is the sound of my true speaking voice. In addition, this is how I will now speak most of the time in my daily life. When I need to speak louder, I simply use my diaphragm to project this deep and significant voice of mine farther.

"And I like the sound of my true voice. I like the sound of my vocal tone. I enjoy hearing the sounds I make as I speak words. I feel relaxed, confident, and powerful and in control just by hearing my deeper resonant voice.

"I imagine now that I am in a public place. As a significant and pleasant tone comes forth from me, those who hear it recognize it as the voice of someone who is confident, self-assured, and authoritative. I do not need to shout or even speak loudly. Others give me more respect as they hear my resonant voice, and this pleases me.

"In the past, my voice may have been shrill or higher pitched at times. It projected uncertainty and timidity I wanted to eliminate from my image ... the image I project to others and myself.

"I choose now to project an image of graceful certainty and self-possession. * I release forever the unconscious habit of speaking in a high, shrill, or thin tone. As I find my true voice, I

The Manifestation Revelation

will not only project a stronger, more confident image, I will begin to feel more powerful and more self-assured.

"If I notice my voice becoming high or shrill or less confident, I will immediately, whether consciously or unconsciously, think of the part of my body below the ribcage: my diaphragm. When I do, my voice will subtly change to a deeper, more authoritative sound. It is my true voice and I will discover myself feeling confident as I speak.

"With my true voice, others listen to me more attentively. My words have more weight to them. It feels good to be really heard.

"I realize now that I feel more confident in my abilities and my rights as an equal to all others. My voice reflects that realization. And from now on I speak in a deeper, stronger voice. *"

(The Wake-Up)

"I will emerge gently and easily from hypnosis now by counting from one to five. With each number, I emerge twenty percent. When I reach the number five, I will return to everyday awareness.

"One . . . emerging twenty percent, beginning to awaken from hypnosis now. (Speak a little louder and stronger.)

"Two . . . forty percent now, as I become fully aware of my body and environment. (Speak louder and stronger.)

"Three . . . sixty percent . . . I look forward to the positive results from this hypnosis session. (Speak louder and stronger.)

"Four . . . eighty percent, emerging peaceful and happy. (Strongly assert your intention to emerge.)

"FIVE . . . FIVE . . . FIVE . . . One hundred percent now! Wide awake and fully alert!!!"

"Emotion Control"

The following suggestions will help you control runaway emotions, such as anger and fear.

"I am ready to gain self-mastery of my feelings. *

"Emotions are wonderful because they add spice to life. Without strong emotions, life would be bland and boring. It is marvelous I am in touch with my emotions. I celebrate and nurture the part of me that feels things strongly, even as I decide now to regulate those emotions.

"I know as an adult how important it is that I access my feelings and learn to control my emotions now. In the past, there were times when my feelings overwhelmed me and I made some bad choices or said things that were inappropriate or even damaging. I see the value of those experiences though, because they taught me why controlling strong emotions such as anger or fear is important.

"By deciding to control and master my emotions, I experience more harmony in relationships, more success while I avoid embarrassment and potential health problems that runaway emotions can cause. Using self-hypnosis to gain control and mastery of my feelings, life becomes immediately happier and better in many ways.

"From now on I automatically monitor and gauge the intensity of my emotions. When a car's engine begins to run too hot, there is a gauge with an indicator to let the driver know. When the indicator reaches toward the red, it warns the driver to attend to its maintenance.

"There have been specific times in my life where I could feel strong emotions beginning to rise and I could feel my internal indicator warning me. From now on, I pay attention to that automatic signal telling me if my emotions are rising toward the red zone.

"As I become aware of my feelings, I can choose to cool my emotions quickly and easily. I take a slow deep breath and I imagine shifting the control lever of my emotions down toward the blue zone. After that, my emotions immediately cool off and I think calmly and rationally about the situation.

"This control works perfectly on any strong emotion I wish to temper, whether it's anger, fear, lust ... I control the level of my emotions now.

"I imagine I'm having a disagreement with someone in my life. As words exchange, I sense my internal gauge indicating that my temper is beginning to rise. While I allow myself to feel and express some appropriate anger, I feel my emotions rising too far toward the red zone. The moment I sense it, I picture myself drawing a slow deep breath while the other person is busy talking. I imagine the control lever of my emotions suspended in the air.

"And as I exhale, I now picture shifting the lever down toward the blue zone. Then I discover the intensity of my anger decreases, giving me continual access to rational thinking and expression. I imagine feeling proud and dignified about the way I handled myself during the disagreement. Self-control feels great!

"At first, I may have to practice this shift. Whenever I practice, I feel a wonderful sense of self-control and mastery, as I can easily reduce the intensity of my feelings to a cool, comfortable blue. Then I will discover, whether expectedly or not, that my mind and body automatically gauge and regulate my emotions within reasonable and manageable limits. Just as an automobile has an automatic cooling system to keep the engine running safely, so too does my mind have its own cooling system.

"And right now, I am adjusting and maintaining that system to work perfectly and automatically through the power of suggestion and self-hypnosis. *"

(The Wake-Up)

"I will emerge gently and easily from hypnosis now by counting from one to five. With each number, I emerge twenty percent. When I reach the number five, I will return to everyday awareness.

"One . . . emerging twenty percent, beginning to awaken from hypnosis now. (Speak a little louder and stronger.)

"Two . . . forty percent now, as I become fully aware of my body and environment. (Speak louder and stronger.)

"Three . . . sixty percent . . . I look forward to the positive results from this hypnosis session. (Speak louder and stronger.)

"Four . . . eighty percent, emerging peaceful and happy. (Strongly assert your intention to emerge.)

"FIVE . . . FIVE . . . FIVE . . . One hundred percent now! Wide awake and fully alert!!!"

"Find Misplaced Objects"

The following script helps you to recall the location of a lost object.

"I want to remember the location of the object. (Think about the object for a moment.)

"My subconscious remembers everything I have ever done. It faithfully records, better than any mechanical device, every event down to the smallest detail. Because it remembers everything, it knows the exact place where I left the object I wish to recover. (Think about that object for a moment.)

"Through the power of self-hypnosis, I request conscious access to the memory of where I last placed or saw the object I wish to recover. What is more, because this is an easy thing for my subconscious mind to do, I relax and allow it to bring this information to my conscious mind. There is no sense of conscious effort required. I request the information, and my subconscious brings it to my awareness because my subconscious is my powerful and efficient friend and ally.

"Right now, with my eyes open, I imagine the mislaid item. I imagine that I have already recovered it. I feel the sense of happiness and relief at being reunited with this object now. Maybe I found it right where I last laid it. Or maybe someone moved it. Either way, I think of it back in my hands and I experience pleasure right now being reunited with it.

"Now that I rediscovered its location, it makes perfect sense to me. Of course, that is where it was! As I look back, I remember knowing exactly the chain of events that brought this item to the place where I found it.

"I find the object. * I'm aware of its current location and that information comes to me. Even now, my subconscious mind locates the image of where I last saw the object. Soon that information becomes available to my conscious mind.

"I now imagine a little bubble. This bubble shows the image of the memory of what happened. It helps me locate the item I am looking for. I pretend that this bubble begins rising from somewhere below the surface of my mind. The memory bubble rises toward the surface ... higher and higher. What is more, when it reaches the surface, I can see in my mind the image on the bubble that reveals the exact location of the object.

"In a short time or even sooner, after emerging from this self-hypnosis session, I will go and recover the object because I remember exactly where it is. All I must do is relax and allow this information to surface. And it does, because my mind knows exactly where to find it now."

(The Wake-Up)

"I will emerge gently and easily from hypnosis now by counting from one to five. With each number, I emerge twenty percent. When I reach the number five, I will return to everyday awareness.

"One . . . emerging twenty percent, beginning to awaken from hypnosis now. (Speak a little louder and stronger.)

"Two . . . forty percent now, as I become fully aware of my body and environment. (Speak louder and stronger.)

"Three . . . sixty percent . . . I look forward to the positive results from this hypnosis session. (Speak louder and stronger.)

"Four . . . eighty percent, emerging peaceful and happy. (Strongly assert your intention to emerge.)

"FIVE . . . FIVE . . . FIVE . . . One hundred percent now! Wide awake and fully alert!!!"

"Forgiveness"

I forgive myself and others of all wrongdoing.

"I ask for and recognize the forgiveness of the Divine as I understand what has always been available to me. In addition, because I freely and totally accept Divine forgiveness, I now freely and totally forgive others for any wrongdoing. Besides, since the Divine is greater than I am, certainly it is acceptable for me to ... forgive myself.

"I release both conscious and unconscious guilt and shame now from all wrong thoughts, words and deeds of the past. What is past is past. It is gone now.

"Furthermore, I am a different person now than I was then. I have more understanding, for I am a growing and developing human being. I am ready now to move on to become even better, unburdened by guilty thoughts and feelings—so I dissolve them. They no longer serve any useful purpose because I forgive myself completely now.

"In turn, I now forgive all persons who have ever harmed me in any way, whether intentionally or unintentionally. Since I know that the Divine forgives me, it is easy to forgive myself and to forgive others. Therefore, I forgive them. I forgive all persons or groups of people from the depths of my being.

"People do hurtful and immature things sometimes. I have done them; I've known other people who have as well. It only makes sense to forgive myself and others about hurting people. It makes little difference to me why they hurt me or even how often they did. I have hurt others more than once with no good reason. Therefore, if the Divine forgives me and I forgive myself, I now extend that same forgiveness to those who have hurt me.

"Holding on to anger and resentment toward others keeps me from moving forward in my life. It keeps me from experiencing more joy and love. It keeps a part of me in bondage to the past. I want to be free. I am ready to let go of all resentment I feel toward anyone who hurt me in the past ... so I can live more joyfully and abundantly.

"I allow my mind to bring to me those who have hurt me ... one by one (pause and think) ... And as each person comes to my mind, I imagine that there is a heavy metal chain that is painfully binding the two of us together. As I feel and utter the words, 'I release you and wish you well', I imagine the chains breaking and dissolving entirely and releasing us both from bondage. * I imagine them walking away from me, free and smiling.

"And with this forgiveness, I realize that I am free also! I am free of anything that used to hold me back. I am free to move forward. I am free to express greater love toward myself, toward others and to the Divine.

"From now on when I think of myself, I see a person learning and growing. When I see other people, I know that they, too, are learning and growing in their own way and in their own time. And when I think of the Divine, I realize that any obstructions between us have been cleared ... like a clear freshwater pond. I am free and clear now."

(The Wake-Up)

"I will emerge gently and easily from hypnosis now by counting from one to five. With each number, I emerge twenty percent. When I reach the number five, I will return to everyday awareness.

"One . . . emerging twenty percent, beginning to awaken from hypnosis now. (Speak a little louder and stronger.)

"Two . . . forty percent now, as I become fully aware of my body and environment. (Speak louder and stronger.)

"Three . . . sixty percent . . . I look forward to the positive results from this hypnosis session. (Speak louder and stronger.)

"Four . . . eighty percent, emerging peaceful and happy. (Strongly assert your intention to emerge.)

"FIVE . . . FIVE . . . FIVE . . . One hundred percent now! Wide awake and fully alert!!!"

"Get Out of Bed in the Morning"

This script motivates you to rise from bed after sleeping. For best results, use before bedtime.

"I want to get out of bed effortlessly and eagerly after sleeping.

"When I wake up in the morning at the appointed time, I feel refreshed and emerge from bed quickly and easily. *

"I program my mind now to grant me a very restful sleep. When my sleeping hours are over and it is time to continue with my waking life, my subconscious prompts both my mind and body to safely awaken and to get out of bed.

"Staying in bed after waking tends to make me feel sluggish and tired. I want to enter my waking day empowered and energized. Therefore, I no longer linger in bed after waking in the morning. Instead, I safely and automatically get out of bed within one minute.

"Each waking day holds a world of good things and opportunities for me. I look forward to partaking in the day as it unfolds. The sooner I arise from bed after waking, the sooner I can start to enjoy both the simple and complex pleasures that only waking life can offer.

"While awake, I appreciate the magic of my senses. While fully awake, I find wonder and satisfaction in everything I see, hear, taste, smell, and touch. Every day offers me the chance to understand my world better, and to understand myself more. Now, that makes it worthwhile to get out of bed in the morning!

"Sleep allows me to rest my body and mind and restore my energy to enjoy the day. Sleep enables me to live my waking hours in a full, healthy, and productive way.

"Those waking hours begin immediately following sleep time. Therefore, within the first minute of awakening from my resting period, I feel a powerful and joyful urge to get out of bed to experience waking life.

"I imagine waking up from sleep. The moment my eyes open and I draw my first waking breath, I realize it is morning now. I have a deep-seated appreciation to experience another waking day.

"I immediately feel in my body a strong urge to sit up in bed and gently stretch my body. I obey my body, and sit up. It is as though my body is telling me that it is finished with its sleep cycle and wants to get up and move about, because my body is made for movement.

"Again, I agree and gently get out of bed. It feels great to get up and out of bed after a good night's sleep. It feels natural that I am eager to enjoy the correct rhythm of life. I look forward now to experience whatever this day holds and make choices that allow me to enjoy my life even more.

"It feels good to get out of bed without delay and start the day immediately after sleeping. And as I do, I feel energetic and enthusiastic about everything I experience."

(The Wake-Up)

"I will emerge gently and easily from hypnosis now by counting from one to five. With each number, I emerge twenty percent. When I reach the number five, I will return to everyday awareness.

"One . . . emerging twenty percent, beginning to awaken from hypnosis now. (Speak a little louder and stronger.)

"Two . . . forty percent now, as I become fully aware of my body and environment. (Speak louder and stronger.)

"Three . . . sixty percent . . . I look forward to the positive results from this hypnosis session. (Speak louder and stronger.)

"Four . . . eighty percent, emerging peaceful and happy. (Strongly assert your intention to emerge.)

"FIVE . . . FIVE . . . FIVE . . . One hundred percent now! Wide awake and fully alert!!!"

"Honoring Your Feminine Self"

This increases feelings of self-worth and self-confidence for the feminine mind and perspective.

"I am ready to feel empowered and joyful about my feminine self.

"I embrace my feminine self as powerful, beautiful and noble. * I dissolve disempowering and limiting thoughts and ideas about femininity and myself. I identify and dismiss male sexism and bias coming from people, media, culture, or religion, and I choose instead to see my feminine self as strong, intelligent, and secure.

"My feminine mind is complex and versatile. * I have vast knowledge and understanding from a perspective the masculine mind cannot readily see. Without my voice and perception, the world is flat, cruel, and ugly. Therefore, I honor the way I think as a woman. I express my observations and viewpoints. My thoughts and opinions have great value.

"My female body is supple and enduring. * It is well known that, on average, women live longer than men. I treasure what is special, lovely, and strong about my feminine body and its functions. I see my body as glorious and beautiful.

"I celebrate my feminine spirit! * I am courageous, nurturing and patient. I courageously nurture my own feelings of high feminine self-esteem and patiently observe how my life changes.

"I imagine now that I am a queen of a magnificent realm. I picture myself sitting upon a throne surrounded by the nobles of my court who await my commands. I hold a scepter in my hand and rule the land with intelligence, justice, and mercy. As a queen, I feel feminine and powerful.

"I allow the feelings of femininity and empowerment to continue hours and days after this session concludes. * I revere and embrace my feminine power and sensibilities. I recognize myself as a woman who is vitally important to her friends, family, community, and world.

"I honor my feminine self and express the joy of being a woman. *"

(The Wake-Up)

"I will emerge gently and easily from hypnosis now by counting from one to five. With each number, I emerge twenty percent. When I reach the number five, I will return to everyday awareness.

"One . . . emerging twenty percent, beginning to awaken from hypnosis now. (Speak a little louder and stronger.)

"Two . . . forty percent now, as I become fully aware of my body and environment. (Speak louder and stronger.)

"Three . . . sixty percent . . . I look forward to the positive results from this hypnosis session. (Speak louder and stronger.)

"Four . . . eighty percent, emerging peaceful and happy. (Strongly assert your intention to emerge.)

"FIVE . . . FIVE . . . FIVE . . . One hundred percent now! Wide awake and fully alert!!!"

"Job Interview Confidence"

This hypnosis suggestion script boosts your confidence and professionalism during job interview.

"I want to be confident as I am interviewed for possible employment. *

"Employers are mostly looking for candidates who are competent, enthusiastic and confident. They get many resumes for a given job. Many applicants have similar credentials. Therefore, often the job interview determines the person they hire.

"When they interview someone for employment, it is primarily to see if the personality and demeanor is a match for the job position. I easily meet and exceed their expectations. *

"I believe in myself. I trust my abilities, my intelligence, and the way I favorably present myself. I recognize myself as a valuable person, perfectly suited to get the job I desire. *

"I present myself in a professional, self-assured and enthusiastic manner during a job interview. I dress and groom myself in a way that reveals my self-respect and my respect for my potential employer. I dress for success for all job interviews, because how I look makes an impression on potential employers. And I want their impression of me to be excellent.

"I make eye contact with the person who interviews me and with everyone I meet throughout the interview process. * I make it known I would enjoy working at their company and I know I would be a great asset to them. I let what is appealing about my personality shine through my words, my facial expressions, and my body language. I smile when appropriate while also demonstrating I take the interview process seriously.

"Whether I consider myself a reserved or an outgoing person, I express my personality during any job interview. My words and responses to questions flow easily and confidently from my mouth. * I speak with a clear, strong voice. I know who I am and that I deserve to be hired. I respectfully and subtly allow this attitude to express itself.

"I imagine now that I am about to be interviewed for employment. I am dressed well to show respect and to present myself as someone to be taken seriously. As the personnel manager comes to greet me, I smile and make strong eye contact.

"As I am invited inside an office for the interview, I feel relaxed, confident and professional. The personnel manager reviews my qualifications and asks me questions. I answer in an audible, clear, and confident voice, continuing to make eye contact.

"As I answer each question, I express my natural personality with poise and professionalism. I feel confident as I ask a few questions about the job and the company. I volunteer that I would like this job and how proud I would feel to work for this company. I confidently reveal why I think I would be of great value to this company.

"As the interview ends, I thank the personnel manager and ask when I can expect to hear whether I have been hired. As I exit the office, I walk away with poise and dignity. Regardless of the outcome, this was a great interview and I feel great about myself!

"As I approach a job interview, I repeat three times to myself aloud or silently, 'Relaxed, confident, professional.'* Whenever I do this, I will experience a boost in confidence and empowerment that lasts throughout the entire interview. * Repeating 'Relaxed, confident, professional' immediately puts me in a self-assured and professional state of mind and body. *

"I am ready to be employed. I make a valuable addition to any company that hires me."

(The Wake-Up)

"I will emerge gently and easily from hypnosis now by counting from one to five. With each number, I emerge twenty percent. When I reach the number five, I will return to everyday awareness.

"One . . . emerging twenty percent, beginning to awaken from hypnosis now. (Speak a little louder and stronger.)

"Two . . . forty percent now, as I become fully aware of my body and environment. (Speak louder and stronger.)

"Three . . . sixty percent . . . I look forward to the positive results from this hypnosis session. (Speak louder and stronger.)

"Four . . . eighty percent, emerging peaceful and happy. (Strongly assert your intention to emerge.)

"FIVE . . . FIVE . . . FIVE . . . One hundred percent now! Wide awake and fully alert!!!"

"Joyful Living"

This script will help you awaken feelings of joy and appreciation for the beauty of life.

"I want to experience the joy of life. *

"It is time for me to feel the wonder and enchantment of life! I am ready to start noticing everything and everyone in my life as sources of marvel, beauty, joy.

"Life is a miracle. And by taking time to appreciate the miracle of even the simplest aspects of daily life, I allow myself to experience blissful appreciation of all that I experience. And it is easy to feel the joy of life ... as I take the time to act on it.

"There are many things I once took for granted—things that have become familiar to me. I forgot to truly recognize the beauty and fascinating qualities of the people, places, and things all around me every day. But now I remember. Now I look for the beauty of all things and easily find it. * And when I see beauty, joy grows inside me.

"My body and all its functions are amazing. My ability to see, to taste, to hear, to touch and to smell are incredible and mysterious. I delight in all my senses and use them to stir up the joy I feel. I take time to notice the banquet of experiences my senses allow me to have.

"Even at this moment, I can feel the richness of life. My hands touch and hold these images before me, and I take time to notice that sensation now. With my eyes, I can read these words and understand them. I can hear my own one-of-a-kind voice, which allows me to express myself however I wish.

"The complexity involved in this experience reveals the wealth of life's riches I enjoy every day of my life. So, I will take time to enjoy my senses as I go about my day and fully experience the joy of life, as though each activity were special and magical—because life is special and magical. All I need to do is observe and enjoy!

"There are magnificent and precious people in my life. Whether they are family, friends, co-workers, or strangers, each individual I encounter is a living miracle. And observing and contemplating that is an instant source of joy to me.

"I now imagine that I am an alien from a faraway planet who has just arrived on earth and is experiencing everything for the first time. I have been lent this spectacular human body with all its senses and abilities to observe this wondrous planet. I find great novelty and delight in the colors and vibrancy of flowers and foliage. The sight of animals and even insects is glorious to behold. I talk to other human beings and I experience their unique personalities and appearances. As I move about each day, this entire experience feels exotic and full of energy to me. Indeed, there is joy in this human experience.

"I experience now the joy and beauty of living. I recognize the wonder of every activity and life experience. I am both a full participant and full observer of the joy of living. I revel in the power of my human body and the experiences it allows me to have. And most of all, I have joy in my ability to think, feel and love. *"

(The Wake-Up)

"I will emerge gently and easily from hypnosis now by counting from one to five. With each number, I emerge twenty percent. When I reach the number five, I will return to everyday awareness.

"One . . . emerging twenty percent, beginning to awaken from hypnosis now. (Speak a little louder and stronger.)

"Two . . . forty percent now, as I become fully aware of my body and environment. (Speak louder and stronger.)

"Three . . . sixty percent . . . I look forward to the positive results from this hypnosis session. (Speak louder and stronger.)

"Four . . . eighty percent, emerging peaceful and happy. (Strongly assert your intention to emerge.)

"FIVE . . . FIVE . . . FIVE . . . One hundred percent now! Wide awake and fully alert!!!"

"Lighten Up!"

*This script encourages a happy mood by
letting go of burdensome thoughts.*

"I lighten up my mood and enjoy life much more now! *

"I enjoy a lightness of being and I see the wonders and beauty of life that is all around me every day. I have fun with the tasks and chores of life, recognizing them as opportunities for me to ... feel more alive. I now discover that physical and seemingly small tasks remind me of the joy of moving my body. I undertake all physical tasks with enthusiasm and lightness of heart. *

"I realize more fully with every passing day that life is like a banquet that I enjoy and treasure. * I relax and have fun with the relationships I have, and choose to ... focus on positive and uplifting aspects ... of those relationships. I bring light and fun to all my relationships and I see others as little children who need to be liked and enjoyed.

"I stop taking myself so seriously starting right now. Yes, starting right now I recognize that the difficulties of life are all part of a great amusement park roller coaster ride. It is the experience of living, and I choose to have fun with my experience during each phase of my life.

"I now imagine that I am in a fun house at an amusement park. I am there with other people I know and care about, and we are having a great time. Everything in the funhouse is there to enjoy ... and makes me feel and see things ... with a lighthearted attitude ...

and to make me laugh ... at the way I look and feel ... as I experience things.

"I see my reflection in the distorted funhouse mirrors. One makes me look two feet tall. One makes me look comically bloated. Another makes me look sometimes squeezed tight and at other times stretched tall ... and I laugh ... at the way I appear ... knowing that it is all in fun ... as I am passing through.

"The funhouse is a metaphor for the way I can choose to respond to difficult situations in my life ... even when things seem wacky or out of place. I choose to lighten up ... the way I do in a funhouse ... and even laugh at life ... or the way I appear ... to myself or others. I have a good time with it ... no longer taking things too seriously ... instead, choosing to enjoy the twists and turns that show up in my life.

"I walk, think, act and talk with a lightness of heart. I move like someone who is happy and full of vigor and joy. I think lighthearted thoughts and I speak lighthearted comments. *

"As I lighten up now, things that once bothered me and made me feel small, squeezed or stretched ... now make me shrug my shoulders and laugh. And it feels good ... just to be able to enjoy my life ... with a lighter heart now. It keeps me happier, brighter, and more joyful. That's a good way to go through life."

(The Wake-Up)

"I will emerge gently and easily from hypnosis now by counting from one to five. With each number, I emerge twenty percent. When I reach the number five, I will return to everyday awareness.

"One . . . emerging twenty percent, beginning to awaken from hypnosis now. (Speak a little louder and stronger.)

"Two . . . forty percent now, as I become fully aware of my body and environment. (Speak louder and stronger.)

"Three . . . sixty percent . . . I look forward to the positive results from this hypnosis session. (Speak louder and stronger.)

"Four . . . eighty percent, emerging peaceful and happy. (Strongly assert your intention to emerge.)

"FIVE . . . FIVE . . . FIVE . . . One hundred percent now! Wide awake and fully alert!!!"

"Lucky Me!"

This script instills the belief that you are a lucky person. The idea is that when you accept and believe this, it will become our manifest reality!

"I am a lucky person. *

"I am now a lucky human being. * All fortunate things come to me as if I were a luck magnet. I am a luck magnet. * I draw to me wonderful experiences that remind me of what a lucky person I really am. * I am lucky.

"I imagine walking in a meadow full of clover. I look down and right away spot a four-leaf clover. I pick up the four-leaf clover and take it with me. It reminds me that I am lucky.

"I picture walking on a sidewalk. As I look down, something shiny catches my eye. It is a lucky penny. I pick up the lucky penny and take it with me. It reminds me that I am a very lucky individual ... because lucky things happen to me all the time.

"I fantasize entering a raffle. The number picked from hundreds of entries is mine! I hear the number. I have won! I feel lucky. And this is the way I am all the time. It is as though I am a magnet for lucky experiences. And it is fun to be as lucky as I am. I am lucky.

"I realize now that as I accept that I am a lucky person the universe around me will act on that realization and send to me even more lucky experiences. I choose to believe and accept that I am lucky. I am destined for lucky experiences. And the universe answers me by sending me luck in life and all my endeavors. * It sends me the right people and circumstances to make my fondest wishes come true.

"And I realize that the four-leaf clover, the shiny penny and the winning raffle number are inside of me. Luck begins inside of me, inside my own thinking and feeling processes. I embrace my luckiness. I absorb the idea that I will be lucky in all my endeavors.

"I know that my mind is very powerful. And I recognize that my subconscious has hidden abilities to draw more luck to me. As I decide that I have this ability and that I am a lucky person, my subconscious will use its hidden abilities to manifest more luck in my daily life."

(The Wake-Up)

"I will emerge gently and easily from hypnosis now by counting from one to five. With each number, I emerge twenty percent. When I reach the number five, I will return to everyday awareness.

"One . . . emerging twenty percent, beginning to awaken from hypnosis now. (Speak a little louder and stronger.)

"Two . . . forty percent now, as I become fully aware of my body and environment. (Speak louder and stronger.)

"Three . . . sixty percent . . . I look forward to the positive results from this hypnosis session. (Speak louder and stronger.)

"Four . . . eighty percent, emerging peaceful and happy. (Strongly assert your intention to emerge.)

"FIVE . . . FIVE . . . FIVE . . . One hundred percent now! Wide awake and fully alert!!!"

"More Faith in the Divine"

This script increases faith and reverence for the Divine.

"I enjoy an ever-stronger faith in the Divine. *

"My rapport with the Divine is very strong. My belief in the Divine Creator and my connection to the Source of all things grows stronger and stronger with every passing day.

"I see the hand of the Divine in all I do, guiding me, and protecting me. * I feel the Divine Presence in each breath I take, and in every sound of life. I grow increasingly aware of the Divine Presence in and around me even now.

"My faith is more than belief. It is a strong force that connects me to what I believe ... and I believe in the Divine. I believe in Divine Love, Divine Wisdom, and Divine Truth. I connect with the Divine in all these aspects and many others on all levels of my mind and body.

"This faith of mine is more than simple doctrine, more than dogma. It goes beyond the words and constructs of human beings. The Divine is real. The Divine Presence becomes ever more real to me with every passing thought. I realize the Divine in ever-greater measure in all that is, and all that I do.

"I am open to receive more Divine Love, Wisdom and Truth in my mind and in my life. I pay attention to the subtle messages the Divine sends me daily that confirm my faith and my truth.

"Yet I am open to change, because the Divine changes me, transforming me into the fullness of being that is intended for me. And as I change, I become wiser and more loving to all in my sphere of influence.

"I take a minute now before awakening from this session to just rest and feel the Divine Presence, so my faith may bask in the experience."

(Take a minute and contemplate your faith in the Divine.)

(The Wake-Up)

"I will emerge gently and easily from hypnosis now by counting from one to five. With each number, I emerge twenty percent. When I reach the number five, I will return to everyday awareness.

"One . . . emerging twenty percent, beginning to awaken from hypnosis now. (Speak a little louder and stronger.)

"Two . . . forty percent now, as I become fully aware of my body and environment. (Speak louder and stronger.)

"Three . . . sixty percent . . . I look forward to the positive results from this hypnosis session. (Speak louder and stronger.)

"Four . . . eighty percent, emerging peaceful and happy. (Strongly assert your intention to emerge.)

"FIVE . . . FIVE . . . FIVE . . . One hundred percent now! Wide awake and fully alert!!!"

"Neat Freak"

This script encourages the user to become more neat and tidy.

"I now choose to be neat and tidy in every aspect of life. *
"I clean and organize my environment regularly, methodically and thoroughly. I find great pleasure in cleaning and straightening things, because it makes me feel clean and organized emotionally and mentally. When my environment is neat and tidy, it makes me feel neat and tidy in my life. * I recognize that there are fringe benefits to cleaning and tidying up.

"I take pride in my appearance, and make sure that I am neat, clean and well put together. This lets me put my best foot forward, whether professionally or socially. I come to understand that my appearance does reflect on me and even affects how I feel about myself. I make every effort to have a neat and purposeful appearance.

"I clean and organize my workspace on a regular basis. * Whether it is a desk, a table, a counter, I have a strong desire to keep it clean, neat, and orderly. It bothers me if it looks messy or unclean for any length of time. And, I find myself cleaning my workspace quite often.

"I clean and organize my living space regularly now. It gives me a feeling of pride and peace to clean and organize my living space. It is as though my living space and my being are linked, and that the condition of my living space affects me. I straighten and clean it often and find that I feel better in my body and my mind. I get a sense of peace as I straighten and clean. And when I'm finished I feel a wonderful sense of accomplishment and satisfaction.

"I symbolically straighten and organize my life affairs, including finances and relationships. I regularly maintain them with care and precision so they work for me. As I clean and straighten my physical environment, I simultaneously purify and clarify my thoughts so my life becomes more orderly. I take pride in my environment and in my life."

(The Wake-Up)

"I will emerge gently and easily from hypnosis now by counting from one to five. With each number, I emerge twenty percent. When I reach the number five, I will return to everyday awareness.

"One . . . emerging twenty percent, beginning to awaken from hypnosis now. (Speak a little louder and stronger.)

"Two . . . forty percent now, as I become fully aware of my body and environment. (Speak louder and stronger.)

"Three . . . sixty percent . . . I look forward to the positive results from this hypnosis session. (Speak louder and stronger.)

"Four . . . eighty percent, emerging peaceful and happy. (Strongly assert your intention to emerge.)

"FIVE . . . FIVE . . . FIVE . . . One hundred percent now! Wide awake and fully alert!!!"

"Okay to Be Gay"

This script assists gay men and women to accept their sexual orientation.

"It is completely okay for me to be gay. *

"Same-sex orientation is a healthy variation of sexuality found in nature. It happens in many species of animals as well as in human beings. Homosexual behavior and couplings have been documented in hundreds of animal species, including many creatures of the seas and lakes, dolphins, zebras, lions, and gorillas. As human beings, we are a part of nature. Therefore, it is logical and wise to consider my own same-sex orientation as part of the natural order of things.

"I love myself and embrace my sexual orientation despite objections from individuals or groups of people. Whether their objections stem from their interpretation of their religion, personal preferences or from deep seated fears regarding their own sexuality, I reject any judgment or criticisms regarding my homosexual orientation and behavior.

"Others have a right to their opinions, and I have the right to discard those opinions. The views of others represent neither facts nor the judgment of the Divine. People think and believe all sorts of erroneous, false, negative, and judgmental things. I disallow their views to harm the way I feel about myself in any way.

"Instead, I acknowledge, accept and decide to appreciate my same-sex orientation. I know who I am and the way I feel. I understand my sexuality better than someone with a different orientation does. I decide what is right and good for me. And I choose to love myself, embrace my same-sex romantic and sexual nature and move forward confidently with my life, attracted, and loving whom I choose. *

"I imagine right now that there are derogatory words written in magic marker all over my body. These are words prejudiced people have used to describe me or gay people—words such as FAG, QUEER, BULLDYKE, HOMO as well as words or phrases that describe sexual activities between gay people in a demeaning way.

"And now I see myself standing beneath a gentle, healing waterfall. As the water cascades over my head and over my body, the black ink of those hurtful and demeaning words begins to smear and smudge away until they are not readable. Then my skin becomes clean as the water washes the last of the ugly ink away entirely. In addition, I feel cleansed of all harmful comments and opinions about my orientation. *

"Instead, I allow life, love and all thoughts about myself and my attraction to my own gender to run free and clear, like that pure, healing water from the waterfall. Now the healing water goes down ... down beneath the surface of my skin ... healing my entire body, mind, and soul of all feelings of shame and guilt about my natural gay orientation.

"Who I choose to reveal my orientation to and what I choose to do with my sexuality is my own choice. Sexual conduct between consenting adults is their own business. Just because some people are uncomfortable with this idea of love does not make adult consensual love wrong or immoral. Therefore, I decide what is appropriate for me. I form my own opinion of my sexuality and my own code of conduct in line with my values. It is okay to be gay.

"Whether it is an evolutionary expression of genetics or a psychological manifestation of a person's upbringing, gay people exist in every culture and in every nation in the world.

"I am part of a dignified sexual minority and have a distinctive perspective of life that only gay people can possess. And with every passing day I increasingly recognize my gay orientation as a wonderful and precious gift. I honor this gift and myself as special."

(The Wake-Up)

"I will emerge gently and easily from hypnosis now by counting from one to five. With each number, I emerge twenty percent. When I reach the number five, I will return to everyday awareness.

"One . . . emerging twenty percent, beginning to awaken from hypnosis now. (Speak a little louder and stronger.)

"Two . . . forty percent now, as I become fully aware of my body and environment. (Speak louder and stronger.)

"Three . . . sixty percent . . . I look forward to the positive results from this hypnosis session. (Speak louder and stronger.)

"Four . . . eighty percent, emerging peaceful and happy. (Strongly assert your intention to emerge.)

"FIVE . . . FIVE . . . FIVE . . . One hundred percent now! Wide awake and fully alert!!!"

"Overcome Alcohol"

This script assists in the complete quitting of drinking beverages containing alcohol.

"I am ready to stop drinking alcohol. *

"I am ready now to stop drinking beverages containing alcohol finally. I have decided taking in alcohol is not good for my body, mind, or life. I make the decision to walk away from alcohol altogether. I already feel a tremendous sense of pride about my decision now to live alcohol-free!

"I already know how unhealthy drinking alcohol is. It turns a healthy liver into one that is scarred and enlarged. The good news is that since I have decided to become alcohol-free now, my liver will heal completely!

"And the same thing is true for other areas of my life that have been damaged by alcohol. By making this revolutionary decision to stop drinking alcohol of any kind, my brain will return to its normal and optimum functioning. My moods will become even and my outlook will be optimistic. My memory will be stronger than ever! My sex drive and potency will recharge! My relationships with loved ones and associates will get much better. I will become the real me as I now become alcohol-free!

"Of course, I may have my own special reasons for deciding to live alcohol-free now. My reasons are personal and very compelling. I take a moment to think of why I have made this decision and what it will mean to me to live alcohol-free (take a moment and think of your reasons) . . .

"I have all the right reasons for discontinuing the behavior of drinking alcohol. I may wonder why I ever drank alcohol in the first place. People sometimes drink as part of a social ritual. Some drink because of the taste of certain beverages. Some drink to become less inhibited with people. Some drink because it seems to relax their minds or bodies. Others drink alcohol to avoid feeling bad.

"Whatever reasons I had for drinking alcohol, I can find healthy and superior ways for fulfilling my needs. For instance, I can take part in any social or cultural ritual by simply choosing or requesting an alcohol-free beverage. I can select very delicious non-alcoholic drinks to enjoy whether I am at home or in social situations to satisfy my taste buds.

"If I think back to when I was a child and first tasted alcohol, I remember that it burned my lips and throat and tasted simply awful! If I had it to do over, I would have chosen to drink something else without any alcohol. Now, as an adult, I make the choice to take in delicious alcohol-free drinks when I am in the mood for something delicious.

"If I ever drank alcohol to become more social, I discover now that I feel relaxed, talkative and interesting all by myself. Alcohol really does not make anyone more fun or interesting. It just distorts the personality and makes people act ridiculous. I am an adult now and I can decide to be myself at parties or in social circumstances. From now on, if I want to become more relaxed and sociable, I will take a sip of any alcohol-free beverage of my choice.

"And when I swallow, I automatically discover my lips are looser and I automatically relax and want to talk. In addition, as I talk I feel good about what I am saying and how I am saying it. The drunken effects of alcohol no longer slur my words. Now that I am alcohol-free, all my words make sense and that makes me want to be even more social.

"Of course, some people drink alcohol just to reduce physical or mental stress. However, there are many ways to relax. Some

The Manifestation Revelation

people choose to take a hot bath. Others choose to exercise. Some learn the relaxing art of meditation. Alternatively, I can even choose to practice self-hypnosis as I am doing right now. And I will discover I feel relaxed physically and mentally. Whatever healthy form of relaxation I choose to practice, I quickly find that it is far superior to the dizzying and muddy sensations of alcohol. I look forward to finding this new healthy way to relax and relieve stress.

"And if I ever drank alcohol to suppress any bad feelings about myself or my life, or to avoid things that I should deal with, I recognize now that it was a poor strategy. I can never hide from myself and I have no need to. I can let go of feelings of shame, guilt, or low self-esteem by forgiving myself and moving forward. If I need others to help me sort out these feelings, I will seek the counsel of a psychologist, a trusted member of the clergy or even a very good friend. When I let go of all anger and sorrow toward myself or other persons ... or even life itself ... I discover what a wonderful person I really am. Then I realize I do not need to feel bad at all. There is no reason to hide from my feelings any longer.

"Now I imagine standing in front of a table with open bottles of what were once my alcoholic beverages of choice. Curiously, I notice there is a photograph of me lying flat on the table partly submerged in a pool of alcohol. As I look at it, I start to feel utterly disgusted as I notice it is my face looking back at me from the watery reflection in the alcoholic liquid—in a kind of double-image. I am sickened with disgust. I notice there are circles under my bloodshot eyes and I have a stupid and drugged expression on my face. I am really prepared to go the other way now!

"I turn my back and walk away from the sad picture and the bottles of alcohol on the soiled table. They get farther and farther away, and smaller and smaller until they become a blurry dot in the distance.

"Then I approach a beautiful table with fine, clean-white linens and lots of bottles of water and other thirst-quenching beverages. There are people I care about surrounding the table who smile and welcome me. I select one of the non-alcoholic drinks and drink it.

"We talk, laugh and have a great time. I feel so comfortable within my own skin. Most of all, I feel a terrific sense of self-esteem and accomplishment—because I have changed my life by walking away from alcohol.

"I know that my subconscious mind is very powerful. Through self-hypnosis I can direct my subconscious mind to change my behavior in positive and beneficial ways. Therefore, as I shortly emerge from self-hypnosis, I fully activate the power of the suggestions to remain alcohol-free. The changes will manifest quickly and without effort."

(The Wake-Up)

"I will emerge gently and easily from hypnosis now by counting from one to five. With each number, I emerge twenty percent. When I reach the number five, I will return to everyday awareness.

"One . . . emerging twenty percent, beginning to awaken from hypnosis now. (Speak a little louder and stronger.)

"Two . . . forty percent now, as I become fully aware of my body and environment. (Speak louder and stronger.)

"Three . . . sixty percent . . . I look forward to the positive results from this hypnosis session. (Speak louder and stronger.)

"Four . . . eighty percent, emerging peaceful and happy. (Strongly assert your intention to emerge.)

"FIVE . . . FIVE . . . FIVE . . . One hundred percent now! Wide awake and fully alert!!!"

"Overcome Depression"

This script helps those with minor depression by using positivism and imagery. There is hope from skilled people who want to relieve you from this unbearable pain.

(Note: If you are suicidal or feel bad for over two months, see a licensed mental health professional.)

"I overcome feelings of depression. *

"I fill my mind with happy and light feelings. I concentrate my attention on whatever is beautiful and full of life. In addition, as I concentrate on these things, my feelings and thoughts transform so that I feel wonderful and good about life and about myself.

"Love and joy overcome depression. I search for ways to love. * I find that I can give love to people, animals, or any living thing. I give them love by serving them in big or small ways. As I serve them out of love, I find that my thoughts and feelings lift and I am full of vigor and enthusiasm.

"I find little tasks of life enjoyable. As I go about my day, I give full attention and interest to the little chores. As I do, I find what is enjoyable about them. I find I take pleasure in the little tasks of life, as well as the bigger tasks. Furthermore, as I decide to fully take part in every task, I find that my attitudes, my feelings, and thoughts rise above all the disheartening thoughts.

"Things of splendor make me feel wonderful. Therefore, I make every effort to surround myself with things of beauty whenever and wherever possible. Even the magnificence of a colorful flower brings to me a feeling of joy and peace. As I concentrate on the beauty of the flower, my feelings immediately lift and remain that way for if I want. I want to feel good. I want to feel happy, alive and enriched. Therefore, I permit myself the experience of feeling wonderful as I put my attention onto beautiful things.

"Now I am thinking of people, places or things I love. They come to my mind easily. I notice as I continue to think of what I love, I begin to realize that I feel much better. As I remember this love, my state of mind grows brighter and brighter ... like the light bulbs attached to a dimmer switch being turned up to make the room brighter and lighter. That is the way thinking about the people, places, or things I love make me feel.

"My new state of mind turns up the dimmer switch making the room of my mind light and bright. It is a great feeling! I can access the feeling any time I wish by simply thinking about it. I can even imagine turning the knob of the dimmer switch to make this love and my state of mind brighter and clearer. I use this technique anytime I want to, any time I need to. And it works better and better each time I use it."

(The Wake-Up)

"I will emerge gently and easily from hypnosis now by counting from one to five. With each number, I emerge twenty percent. When I reach the number five, I will return to everyday awareness.

"One . . . emerging twenty percent, beginning to awaken from hypnosis now. (Speak a little louder and stronger.)

"Two . . . forty percent now, as I become fully aware of my body and environment. (Speak louder and stronger.)

"Three . . . sixty percent . . . I look forward to the positive results from this hypnosis session. (Speak louder and stronger.)

"Four . . . eighty percent, emerging peaceful and happy. (Strongly assert your intention to emerge.)

"FIVE . . . FIVE . . . FIVE . . . One hundred percent now! Wide awake and fully alert!!!"

"Overcome Fear of Failure"

This script helps to end the fear of failure.

"I want to overcome fear of failure. *

"I am now ready to completely dissolve any conscious or unconscious fear of failure from my mind.

"I act to accomplish my goals. I do my best to find the most reasonable course of action and then take the necessary steps toward success. I realize there may be unforeseen challenges that arise, but I trust myself to deal with those intelligently. Any setback or challenge only increases my knowledge and understanding of what is required to bring my goals to full manifestation.

"Most people of great achievement encountered failure on their paths to success. If Thomas Edison had stopped after his many failures, he would have never succeeded in finally inventing the light bulb. Of course, he experienced frustrations along the way. He may have endured the ridicule or envy of others. But his persistence and resolve to see his project successful was stronger than his frustration or embarrassment.

"I easily release worry about experiencing failures on my way to success. * It is okay if there are frustrations on my path to achievement. And what others think of me is unimportant. I replace that fear of failure with a new expectation of discovering how strong, resourceful, and intelligent I truly am.* Because if my projects do not work out the way I want, I can analyze the problems and be persistent until I am successful.

"The only real failure is not to act. Any step toward my goal takes me closer and closer to its completion. I move forward with my plans, taking things one-step at a time. And I enjoy the process.

"There is something important in my life I want to do. I know it will take planning, thought and action to make it happen. I realize that taking the necessary measures to see my desire fulfilled gives me great satisfaction. The joy is in the journey!

"There are several unanticipated challenges that come as I take this journey. Nevertheless, I find
that the challenges are interesting and that they provoke thought. As I find ways to overcome those temporary obstacles, I feel even more confident about myself, about my intelligence and about my ability to accomplish what I want. This greater belief and self-knowledge allows me to accomplish even greater things in the future.

"I imagine before me a great door, a door that leads to my success. Beside it is a great big block of ice. Inside the ice is a golden key to unlock the door. The key represents my ability to act. The ice represents my fear of failure. As I say aloud with conviction, 'I dissolve the fear of failure,' the ice begins to melt away. And as I say, 'My belief in my intelligence and abilities grows stronger,' the ice even cracks.

"When I speak the words, 'I am ready to move forward and face all challenges,' the remaining ice completely melts, leaving behind only the golden key.

"As I pick up the golden key, I realize I now can move forward. Now I put the key in the lock of the great door and turn it. The door opens with a mystical force, and I take a step through the door toward the completion of my goal.

"The fear of failure has melted away completely. And I can move forward with my plans."

(The Wake-Up)

"I will emerge gently and easily from hypnosis now by counting from one to five. With each number, I emerge twenty percent. When I reach the number five, I will return to everyday awareness.

"One . . . emerging twenty percent, beginning to awaken from hypnosis now. (Speak a little louder and stronger.)

"Two . . . forty percent now, as I become fully aware of my body and environment. (Speak louder and stronger.)

"Three . . . sixty percent . . . I look forward to the positive results from this hypnosis session. (Speak louder and stronger.)

"Four . . . eighty percent, emerging peaceful and happy. (Strongly assert your intention to emerge.)

"FIVE . . . FIVE . . . FIVE . . . One hundred percent now! Wide awake and fully alert!!!"

"Reduce Smoking Easily"

This script helps you easily reduce smoking 80% or more within a one-week period. Use it up to seven days before you use the "Stop Smoking Finally" script.

"I acknowledge right now and after this session that reducing smoking is within my power. It is as easy as a simple decision. I admit to myself it's an easy matter for me to reduce smoking approximately 20% each day. That means if I smoked 10 cigarettes yesterday, I smoke eight today. If I smoked eight today, I may only smoke six tomorrow. And so on.

"It is easy and gratifying to smoke just a little less each day. And in about a week or so, after my first reading of this script, I'll have easily reduced my smoking about 80%. * I'll then decide whether I am ready to stop smoking altogether!

"As I see how easy it really is to cut down on smoking, it becomes clear I have much more control than I thought I had. In addition, I understand now that quitting is not only possible, but also very reasonable, logical, and remarkably easy for me.

"I have acted as though cigarettes are in control of me. However, I know that is not true. The truth is I am in control. * The only reason I haven't quit smoking is because I didn't really want to. I pretended smoking had some sort of ridiculous power over me. It does not though. Cigarettes or any kind of tobacco has absolutely no hold over me. *

"I can relax all by myself, like I am doing right now with self-hypnosis ... and I do not even want a cigarette right now. I am relaxed and happy doing something else. I can choose to relax and feel good, and take breaks during my day without wanting a cigarette.

"Cigarettes are a poor substitute for the true feelings of self-acceptance and confidence. I choose to immediately cultivate and nurture feelings of self-worth, self-confidence, and self-acceptance.

"After the session is over, I can decide to say 'No' to a cigarette. And when I do, and every time I say 'No' to a cigarette, I notice how proud of myself I feel ... because I am recognizing my own power and ability to be in control of myself. Saying 'No' to smoking a single cigarette gives me a strong feeling of freedom. I have always had this power, but this hypnosis session is reminding me of that.

"I'm not going to insist that I stop smoking altogether right away. If I make a choice to smoke a cigarette, I can choose so. However, the choice will be clearly and freely mine. I will have a moment when I can freely decide whether to smoke or whether to say 'No' for now and save it for later. Or I can just decide not to smoke at all. Each time I say 'No', I'll notice how good I feel ... and how confident, healthy and empowered I feel. *

"Instead of smoking, I'll take a few deep proud breaths of clean, fresh air and feel the relaxation that comes with that. I might reach for a bottle or glass of water instead of smoking and when I sip the water, it will remind me of what a healthy thing I am doing for myself.

"I find it easy to reduce smoking right now. Every day I find it easier to reduce the number of cigarettes I smoke at least 20%. In less than one week's time I will have reduced the amount I smoke about 80%."

(The Wake-Up)

"I will emerge gently and easily from hypnosis now by counting from one to five. With each number, I emerge twenty percent. When I reach the number five, I will return to everyday awareness.

"One . . . emerging twenty percent, beginning to awaken from hypnosis now. (Speak a little louder and stronger.)

"Two . . . forty percent now, as I become fully aware of my body and environment. (Speak louder and stronger.)

"Three . . . sixty percent . . . I look forward to the positive results from this hypnosis session. (Speak louder and stronger.)

"Four . . . eighty percent, emerging peaceful and happy. (Strongly assert your intention to emerge.)

"FIVE . . . FIVE . . . FIVE . . . One hundred percent now! Wide awake and fully alert!!!"

"Remember Past Lives"

This script encourages the recovery of past life memories in dreams. For best results, read this script right before bedtime.

"I want to remember who I was in my former lifetimes. *

"My dreams can and will recall to me who I was in previous lives. As I go to sleep this very night, I will have one or more dreams that are direct memories of my life in a previous incarnation.

"In addition, when I awaken naturally from sleep, I will remember the dream vividly. I will remember the dreams pertaining to my past lives. I will remember my past lives. *

"My subconscious has access to all my memories, whether in this lifetime or any others I have ever had. These former lives and all my experiences are part of me. They have brought me to who I am, and what I am and what I experience in this lifetime.

"Through my dreams, I wish to safely lift the veil that hides my past life memories from me to understand myself more fully. I wish to learn about my past lives for further self-development in this lifetime.

"I want to know who I was and what happened to grow in my wisdom and self-knowledge. With this intention, I direct my subconscious to reveal safely who I was in one or more previous lifetimes.

"I imagine going to sleep this very night. Soon after, I find I am having a very vivid dream where I am someone else from a previous time. Everything I see and experience in this dream is very familiar to me, because it happened in a previous life. I even catch a glimpse of my face in a mirror or the reflective surface of water. And it is my face from a previous life.

"Everyone I know in the dream is very familiar. They are the people I knew when I lived before.

"As the dream fades, I imagine waking from sleep. The dream is still vivid in my mind. And I write it down in a journal or on a pad of paper to remember it always.

"And I'm intrigued and overjoyed by my dream, because I recognize it revealed a true memory from a past life. Now I can take what I learned about my past life, and understand how things relate to my current circumstances. I can use the dream to make my current life better.

"I have lived before. *

"I have had previous lives. *

"I can safely recall who I was and what I experienced in my past lives. *

"I will dream of who I was and what I experienced in my past lives. *

"I remember my dreams of my past lives. *

"I will experience joy from the self-knowledge I gain."

(The Wake-Up)

"I will emerge gently and easily from hypnosis now by counting from one to five. With each number, I emerge twenty percent. When I reach the number five, I will return to everyday awareness.

"One . . . emerging twenty percent, beginning to awaken from hypnosis now. (Speak a little louder and stronger.)

"Two . . . forty percent now, as I become fully aware of my body and environment. (Speak louder and stronger.)

"Three . . . sixty percent . . . I look forward to the positive results from this hypnosis session. (Speak louder and stronger.)

"Four . . . eighty percent, emerging peaceful and happy. (Strongly assert your intention to emerge.)

"FIVE . . . FIVE . . . FIVE . . . One hundred percent now! Wide awake and fully alert!!!"

"Smile!"

This script encourages smiling as an authentic expression of warmth with old and new acquaintances.

"I now smile more often. *

"Smiling is natural, inviting and disarming. When I smile at people with sincerity, it immediately communicates friendliness and warmth so they are more receptive to me. As I decide to smile more, I will enhance the quality of my relationships, both personal and professional.

"The studies confirm that over 90% of communication is non-verbal. The expressions on my face communicate more than the actual words I use. I now become aware of my facial expressions and prompt myself to smile when I want to communicate sincere warmth or welcome. This will improve my influence and rapport with everyone I know and meet.

"When I greet someone, I let a smile flood all over my face like a warm wave. When I am introduced to a new acquaintance, I reward that person with a cheerful and inviting smile. I also look them directly in the eyes as I smile, letting them know I think they are very special.

"As I smile, I feel a well of gladness rise up from deep within me. That gladness reaches my face and then culminates in a bright, authentic smile. It is as though the sun is rising within me, and my smile lights up my whole face. My smile expresses a feeling of goodwill and happiness.

"As I become aware of my facial expressions and learn to smile more, smiling becomes automatic for me. It becomes my new way of greeting people, whether I know them or not. Smiling is automatic.

"I pretend right now that I am meeting someone for the first time at a social event. As I purposefully make eye contact, I pause for just a moment, then I smile warmly and enthusiastically to let the person know I am glad to meet them.

"I can tell that my smile and sincerity are well received, because naturally the person smiles back at me just as cheerfully. As the conversation continues, I smile whenever appropriate which expresses that I am happy and easy to talk to. I create and develop rapport with my smile. When the conversation is over, I smile again and tell the new acquaintance how wonderful it was to meet them.

"A smile is worth more than many kind words. It expresses so much. And because it's easy to remember to smile, I will use my smile from now on to help communicate and build rapport with others.

"And because smiling on the outside makes me feel good on the inside it is always a pleasurable thing to smile."

(The Wake-Up)

"I will emerge gently and easily from hypnosis now by counting from one to five. With each number, I emerge twenty percent. When I reach the number five, I will return to everyday awareness.

"One . . . emerging twenty percent, beginning to awaken from hypnosis now. (Speak a little louder and stronger.)

"Two . . . forty percent now, as I become fully aware of my body and environment. (Speak louder and stronger.)

"Three . . . sixty percent . . . I look forward to the positive results from this hypnosis session. (Speak louder and stronger.)

"Four . . . eighty percent, emerging peaceful and happy. (Strongly assert your intention to emerge.)

"FIVE . . . FIVE . . . FIVE . . . One hundred percent now! Wide awake and fully alert!!!"

"Stay in the Now"

This script will help you focus on what is happening and keep your mind from wandering.

"I am ready to focus on the here and now. *

"I reserve daydreaming and contemplation of the past or future to times when I am alone and not engaged in any other task. During those times, it is healthy and acceptable for me to allow my mind to relax and wander where it wants. I set aside special and definite periods of time to let my mind drift, recognizing that daydreaming has value.

"Yet when I engage in conversation or in the tasks of life, I decide to remain focused on what I am doing and experiencing. * By staying present and focused, I experience and enjoy my life to a much greater extent. Staying in the now helps me in all areas of my life. *

"I now program and train my mind to stay focused on what is happening in the present. From now on, I become acutely aware anytime my mind wanders from the persons or the tasks. When I my mind wanders, I subtly make a fist with my right hand and squeeze to remind myself to return my attention to the present moment. As I release my fist, my mind returns its focus to the present time.

"I now imagine having a conversation with a friend. In the middle of conversation, as my friend is telling a personal

story, I discover my attention has wandered and I am daydreaming. Because I want to appreciate my friendship and listen to the conversation, I quietly and subtly make a fist with my right hand. As I do, my focus returns to what my friend is saying. My attention completely and fully returns to the present moment.
*

"And after only a short while, I will recognize that staying and focusing in the moment becomes my new habit ... my everyday way of thinking and doing. In addition, I see this making me very happy. My relationships will greatly improve because I learned how to listen and connect with the other person. The tasks that I need to do I will complete with more precision and excellence because I can concentrate on them. Even my joy of daydreaming will improve because I reserve it only for special times when I am alone and when I willingly allow it. And I will be glad that staying in the present has become normal for me."

(The Wake-Up)

"I will emerge gently and easily from hypnosis now by counting from one to five. With each number, I emerge twenty percent. When I reach the number five, I will return to everyday awareness.

"One . . . emerging twenty percent, beginning to awaken from hypnosis now. (Speak a little louder and stronger.)

"Two . . . forty percent now, as I become fully aware of my body and environment. (Speak louder and stronger.)

"Three . . . sixty percent . . . I look forward to the positive results from this hypnosis session. (Speak louder and stronger.)

"Four . . . eighty percent, emerging peaceful and happy. (Strongly assert your intention to emerge.)

"FIVE . . . FIVE . . . FIVE . . . One hundred percent now! Wide awake and fully alert!!!"

"Stop Complaining, Stop Gossiping"

This script reduces complaining and gossiping to express and experience more positivity.

"I want to stop myself from speaking negatively ... I am ready to discontinue gossiping and complaining. *

"From now on, I express and concentrate on all the good in my life. Expressing optimistic and uplifting thoughts ... makes me happier and healthier. I stop myself from speaking negatively. * I let go of misplaced desires to complain or to make unkind remarks about anyone or anything ... because what I really want ... is to feel content about my life and myself.

"As I remember to control the words I speak, it becomes easier to control my thoughts, so even my thoughts now become consistently positive and happy. And as my words and thoughts now become constructive and affirming, I become a happier and healthier person. * I feel better about myself and my life.

"Sharing gossip with others is a form of negative speech. It may come from a misplaced inner need to feel superior to others. I know that gossiping does not make me feel better. It certainly does not make me superior to anyone. From now on, I stop myself from gossiping. * If I catch myself saying anything negative about anyone, I will simply stop in mid-sentence. * I then decide to say something positive and uplifting about that person ... because I see myself as a positive person now.

"I imagine myself right now among a group of friends who are about to gossip about someone we know. Just as I begin to speak negatively about that person—I stop myself. I think about what I am about to say ... and instead, I simply decide to say nothing or I say something positive.

"Because of that positive statement, a wonderful feeling of self-control and self- confidence fills me now. It is a feeling that is much better than the way petty gossip made me feel. It feels good to speak well about other people or just to remain silent. This is my new way of speaking about others.

"I can imagine myself now around a group of friends or business associates who are beginning to gossip. In addition, I discover that even the idea of listening to unkind words about anyone is now completely uncomfortable to me. I quickly excuse myself from their presence and move on to more positive tasks and conversations. I feel a sense of positivity and contentment whenever I remove myself from negative conversations. *

"I stop myself from complaining. * I recognize that most complaining is unnecessary, unpleasant and serves no useful purpose. In the past, I have complained because I felt unhappy or I wanted attention from others.

"From now on, I stop myself from complaining ... because what really makes me happy can never come from complaining about circumstances outside of my control. I act to correct my problems ... and that gives me a feeling of self-reliance and confidence. I replace my need for attention with a proactive and positive approach to people and circumstances. I find that people automatically respect and pay attention to very positive individuals.

"I see myself right now in a situation where once I might have complained. Instead of complaining, I stop myself, and I ponder how to change the negative situation. I know that complaining rarely solves any problems. I decide just to let the complaints dissolve from my mind without expressing them.

"Instead, I now decide to take a long, slow breath.... As I release it, I release all my tension. In addition, as I do I immediately realize how good it feels to take control over my words. That feeling of self-control feels more gratifying than complaining ever could.

"I discontinue gossiping. I discontinue complaining. With every passing hour, I find that my vocal expressions are more positive and kind. * Thus, I feel good about myself, life, and everyone around me. Speaking well of others and circumstances is a beneficial and empowering habit of mine."

(The Wake-Up)

"I will emerge gently and easily from hypnosis now by counting from one to five. With each number, I emerge twenty percent. When I reach the number five, I will return to everyday awareness.

"One . . . emerging twenty percent, beginning to awaken from hypnosis now. (Speak a little louder and stronger.)

"Two . . . forty percent now, as I become fully aware of my body and environment. (Speak louder and stronger.)

"Three . . . sixty percent . . . I look forward to the positive results from this hypnosis session. (Speak louder and stronger.)

"Four . . . eighty percent, emerging peaceful and happy. (Strongly assert your intention to emerge.)

"FIVE . . . FIVE . . . FIVE . . . One hundred percent now! Wide awake and fully alert!!!"

"Stop People Pleasing"

This script encourages the reader to say "No" to people, when appropriate, and it fosters steps to create self-respect and necessary boundaries in relationships.

"I am ready to stop compulsively pleasing people. *

"I now release myself from any conscious or unconscious need to overexert or overextend myself physically or mentally just to please another person.

"The right people will like me and love me even when I choose to say no to their requests. I continue to both love and be loved ... even when I

say no to others. Therefore, I only do things for others when I want to ... when it feels right and appropriate for me to do so.

"And if someone doesn't like me anymore, because I say no to them ... then I have to wonder if they ever really liked me in the first place ... or whether they just liked me for what I did for them.

"From now on, I override any compulsion to please others out of habit, out of guilt or just to gain approval from other people. * Whether in my personal life or in my professional life, I create boundaries with others ... and establish my self-respect. Because as I now learn to respect myself ... and my own time and effort, others must respect me more. * It is only natural.

"There are times when it is in my best interest to serve or help another person or to say yes to a request. There are times when I want to show someone I care about him or her by doing a good or helpful deed or chore for them. In addition, it is all right to help someone out of charity or love.

"However, there are times when helping is a great inconvenience, and I now find I can choose to say no to that request for assistance. I place careful boundaries on my effort and my time.

"I am as important as any other person. I am important. I matter. I matter to me. As my own guardian and friend, I make other people treat me well. * Part of treating me well and protecting me is to recognize I can say no to most requests. Saying no is a way of protecting myself. Saying no establishes important boundaries. These restrictions are right and good for me to establish and maintain with family, friends, coworkers, and employers. Anyone who does not respect my boundaries is unworthy of my respect or time. * I disregard anyone who does not value my borders.

"I imagine being asked by a family member, or friend or coworker to do something that is not an emergency and would greatly inconvenience me. I easily and respectfully tell them 'No.' As the word 'No' comes forth, I immediately feel good about myself. I imagine that the person still respects me, and honors my right to say no to their request. And I imagine that they can find another way or another person to help them.

"I now think about what happens when I say 'no' and the requester seems angry with me. However, I continue to feel very good about my decision. I feel good because I am my own guardian and best friend. It is not my responsibility to comply with all requests made of me. I enjoy setting my limits and guarding those boundaries.

"I am still a good person, even when I say 'No' to people. In fact, it makes me a better person because it proves that I have self-respect. I have limits on what I will do. And this is a very good thing.

"I look forward to saying 'No' to people who make unreasonable demands of me. I calmly but emphatically say 'No, I can't do that' or 'I'm sorry, but I can't help you with that.' And it feels good to say those things aloud."

(The Wake-Up)

"I will emerge gently and easily from hypnosis now by counting from one to five. With each number, I emerge twenty percent. When I reach the number five, I will return to everyday awareness.

"One . . . emerging twenty percent, beginning to awaken from hypnosis now. (Speak a little louder and stronger.)

"Two . . . forty percent now, as I become fully aware of my body and environment. (Speak louder and stronger.)

"Three . . . sixty percent . . . I look forward to the positive results from this hypnosis session. (Speak louder and stronger.)

"Four . . . eighty percent, emerging peaceful and happy. (Strongly assert your intention to emerge.)

"FIVE . . . FIVE . . . FIVE . . . One hundred percent now! Wide awake and fully alert!!!"

"Stop Smoking Finally!"

The following eliminates the behavior of smoking cigarettes and using tobacco.

"I am ready to stop smoking now. *

"I am ready to stop smoking for myself. Smoking is poison to my body and I want to live. Therefore, it is time to choose to live smoke-free. I use the power of hypnosis, suggestion, and imagination to communicate this truth to my subconscious.

"I imagine that I smoke three times as much as I ever did. I see that all the horrible aspects of smoking are three times worse. My breathing feels labored and heavy. My clothes smell constantly of smoke. My stained teeth are soaked with tar. The smoke fills my nostrils and there is an unpleasant sensation in my throat, lungs, and chest. It is a terrible feeling!

"But now I imagine something different.

"I imagine I am smoke-free for many years. And I picture walking along a warm white, sandy beach on a cloudless day. The pure air is crisp and fresh and warm and feels so good. I walk without a care, and am full of energy and vitality. I feel clean and part of nature.

"Would I ever trade these wonderful feelings of cleanliness, vitality and freedom for a lousy cigarette?

"Now I imagine myself in a place where I used to smoke: in the car, after a meal, or on the phone. In addition, I see myself without a cigarette because I am a non-smoker. I am completely smoke-free and feeling great. I am smiling and very proud that I have discarded such a deadly and disgusting habit.

"I see myself with friends. Some of them even smoke in front of me. Nevertheless, it does not bother me. In fact, when they smoke, I feel sorry for them—because they have a bad habit they have not kicked yet. Yet I feel even better about myself; because I recall how completely smoke-free I am and about how my life has dramatically improved as a non-smoker.

"With this feeling of control and empowerment I also discover how easily I control how much I eat. I eat normal portions of healthy food. As I have become a non-smoker, I remain at my current weight, unless I choose to lose weight with my newfound confidence and self-control.

"I feel relaxed and calm without smoking. * I'm more confident and secure than I have ever been. It is like having a completely new life. I discover I do not even want a cigarette anymore. *

"The smell of cigarettes has now become unappealing and the thought of putting one to my mouth is utterly repulsive. Instead, when I want to feel more relaxed and calm throughout my day, I take a break from what I am doing. I find a place where I can draw five to ten slow deep breaths. I let oxygen fill my body and brain, refreshing, and relaxing me naturally ... cleanly. When I do this, it reminds me what a great choice I made to become a happy, healthy non-smoker. It's one of the best things I have ever done.

"I realize smoking didn't make me attractive, 'cool' or special. Cigarettes stained my teeth. I looked very silly sucking from a little white paper tube filled with ugly brown stuff!

"I now think about what it will feel like to be free of cigarettes after this hypnosis session. * The thought of smoking will seem ridiculous and distant ... as if it was someone else who smoked far off and long ago. I embrace my smoke-free identity fully and resolutely. I see myself breathing pure air, drinking lots of clean fresh water and enjoying my new healthy life. The temptation to smoke does not exist, and there will be no withdrawal symptoms whatsoever, because my body accepts its identity as a non-smoker. *

"And now I'm ready to experience my smoke-free life. I am and will remain a non-smoker from this time forward. *"

(The Wake-Up)

"I will emerge gently and easily from hypnosis now by counting from one to five. With each number, I emerge twenty percent. When I reach the number five, I will return to everyday awareness.

"One . . . emerging twenty percent, beginning to awaken from hypnosis now. (Speak a little louder and stronger.)

"Two . . . forty percent now, as I become fully aware of my body and environment. (Speak louder and stronger.)

"Three . . . sixty percent . . . I look forward to the positive results from this hypnosis session. (Speak louder and stronger.)

"Four . . . eighty percent, emerging peaceful and happy. (Strongly assert your intention to emerge.)

"FIVE . . . FIVE . . . FIVE . . . One hundred percent now! Wide awake and fully alert!!!"

"Stop Worrying"

This script provides release from everyday worry habits.

"I release myself from worry. *

"I let go of the heavy burden of worrying about my life, about my relationships and the world around me. Instead, I choose to focus on the present. I concentrate my attention on making the happiest, best decisions I can make for me now. And I allow that decision to be satisfying and sufficient for me.

"I realize that worry is counterproductive and I want to do things that make me happy and peaceful. Therefore, any time I discover myself worrying about anything, I gently and immediately remind myself to return to the present moment and focus on good and helpful things.

"Worry is imaginary. It is a product of the imagination. It is a negative projection of fear and has no basis. Letting go of something that is unpleasant and imaginary is easy for me to do now. *

"I imagine that I am on a beach and carrying heavy bags of sand on my back and shoulders. The bags of sand represent all the worries I have been carrying. They are very heavy and make it very hard for me to move forward. The bags of sand are a heavy burden and I ask myself 'Do I need to carry these worries around?' I instantly recognize the answer is 'No!' Therefore, I now drop the heavy bags of sand. I let go of the heavy burden of worries I was carrying. I release all worrisome thoughts. I let them drop to the ground with a loud 'thunk.'

"The moment I drop them I feel much better, and much lighter, and freer! I can now move forward with ease. I can now do whatever I want and let the worry go.

"I imagine walking along the beach now, happy and light-hearted. I look back and see the bags of sand on the ground far behind me. As I walk farther, the bags are getting smaller and smaller ... smaller and smaller ... until they are just a dot and then a blur. They are far away now that there is no point even looking back.

"I just look forward now. I know I am free to think positive thoughts. I am free to get on with my life and let things happen as they will.

"As I walk on the beach, I see a beautiful sunrise ahead of me. I walk toward that sunrise, feeling light, joyful and free."

(The Wake-Up)

"I will emerge gently and easily from hypnosis now by counting from one to five. With each number, I emerge twenty percent. When I reach the number five, I will return to everyday awareness.

"One . . . emerging twenty percent, beginning to awaken from hypnosis now. (Speak a little louder and stronger.)

"Two . . . forty percent now, as I become fully aware of my body and environment. (Speak louder and stronger.)

"Three . . . sixty percent . . . I look forward to the positive results from this hypnosis session. (Speak louder and stronger.)
"Four . . . eighty percent, emerging peaceful and happy. (Strongly assert your intention to emerge.)

"FIVE . . . FIVE . . . FIVE . . . One hundred percent now! Wide awake and fully alert!!!"

BONUS SECTION

IN THE LAST FEW YEARS, i have made several updates to *Instant Self Hypnosis* that may be of great value to you, particularly if you are an experienced user of the eyes-open method. If you are new, I suggest you first master the basic eyes-open self-hypnosis method before you try any of the techniques in this book's Bonus Section.

Once these basics are familiar and comfortable, you can employ one or more of the techniques contained in this section.

ENHANCE SCRIPT IMPACT

If you want to make your eyes-open self-hypnosis sessions more potent, it is easily accomplished.:

WHILE LOOKING OVER THE 48 SCRIPTS, you may have noticed there are asterisks (*) after some of the hypnotic suggestions. These suggestions are usually of a fundamentally important kind, designed to help you produce the essential change you seek.

Whenever you see an asterisk "" after a suggestion, reread the sentence aloud.*

Then continue reading the script, as usual. Here is an example: If the script reads: "...what others think of me is unimportant. I replace the fear of failure with an expectation of discovering how strong, resourceful and intelligent I truly am * ..." you would repeat the second sentence aloud.

Here is how that part of the script is to be read using this advanced technique:

> * "...what others think of me is unimportant. I replace the fear of failure with an expectation of discovering how strong, resourceful, and intelligent I truly am.* **I replace the fear of**

failure with an expectation of discovering how strong, resourceful, and intelligent I truly am." (The bolded second sentence must be repeated.)

* When you repeat the sentence, you may use the same tone of voice you used when you read first the sentence. Or you may add a bit more emphasis to strengthen the suggestion.

This repetition principle has a compounding effect of making a powerful impression on the subconscious mind. Though it will slightly lengthen the duration of the session, it is well worth it.

DEEPER INSTANT SELF-HYPNOSIS

Experiencing a deeper level of self-hypnosis is easy to do if you do not mind taking an extra few minutes to accomplish it. I have included two deepening scripts here.

EACH DEEPENING SCRIPT SHOULD be read after the Master Induction 2.0 but before reading the script for your goal. You may choose to use just one of the two deepening scripts. On the other hand, if you really want to experience something truly extraordinary, use both deepening scripts (one after the other) before reading the suggestion script you selected.

The first script, the Super Deepening Script, offers a wonderful technique to command more focus and quiet your mind to be more receptive to the upcoming goal suggestions.

The second script, called the Ultra Deepening Script, uses an original mixture of eyes-open and eyes-closed techniques that deeply relaxes the mind and nervous system.

"Super Deepening Script"

(to be read aloud)

"I easily go deeper into self-hypnosis now.

"I'm going to quiet down all the other thoughts and 'voices' in my head and I can relax my mind completely to focus only on this self-hypnosis session.

"I imagine I'm a teacher in the middle of a room full of noisy, chattering children. Some of them are talking nonstop to one another. Some are calling out to get my attention. Others are showing off things they saw on television. Some sing random popular songs they know.

"To get their attention and quiet them down, I say to them: 'It is time to be quiet now and pay attention.' After that, I notice the children who were calling out to me immediately become quiet and attentive.

"Then I put my forefinger to my mouth and gently make the sound 'Shhhh.' The kids who were singing random songs or showing off become calm and attentive. Once more, I slowly draw out the sound, 'Shhhhhhhhhhh.' When I do, the kids stop chattering to one another and pay total attention to me.

"I tell them, 'Very good. I am going to read to you now as you listen. I want you to remain quiet and pay total attention as I read. Okay?' The children nod their heads with understanding, while they remain silent and pay close attention to the words I speak.

"The children represent parts of my still developing mind. And their voices represent the many thoughts they naturally generate. Those parts of my mind are now calm, quiet, relaxed and completely receptive to the hypnotic suggestions as I read them." (Turn to your selected script now and continue reading.)

"Ultra-Deepening Script"

(read aloud)

"I want to go much deeper now.

"In a moment, I will close my eyes and count slowly to three, feeling twice as relaxed with each number. When I reach the number three, I will open my eyes and continue to read and notice how utterly relaxed I have become. (Close your eyes, count to three while relaxing deeper with each number. Then open your eyes and continue.)

"I feel much more mentally relaxed and receptive. In a moment, I will close my eyes again and slowly repeat the phrase 'Deeper relaxed now' three times and use my imagination to relax ten times deeper every time I say that phrase. Then I will open my eyes and continue reading. (Close your eyes, repeat 'Deeper relaxed now', then open your eyes and continue reading.)

"Now I really, really feel wonderfully relaxed and my challenges feel light and easy to master. And I am ready to absorb the suggestions I read now." (Please turn to your selected script.)

RAPID INDUCTION

MANY PEOPLE ASKED whether it is necessary to read the entire Master Induction 2.0 each time, as it becomes monotonous to read repeatedly. After several readings, you will find your mind develops such a conditioned response you will be hypnotized in a matter of only moments after starting! At that point, you will find that you will not need to read the complete 2.0 to hypnotize yourself. Instead, you may read the Rapid Induction Script.

True Story —
"How the Master Induction Affects Me"

Because I have been working with the Master Induction since 1997, whenever I now read the first line I can feel myself going into self-hypnosis almost instantly. My body and mind relaxes immediately and a sensation of utter calm comes over me. Sometimes I even stumble over the words, though I know the words by heart.

If you have used Master Induction 2.0 to hypnotize yourself a minimum of six times, you may effectively use the Rapid Induction Script that follows. It allows you to shorten significantly the total length of your sessions without sacrificing the benefits. Essentially, it is a condensed version of Master Induction 2.0.

"Rapid Induction Script"

(to be read aloud)

"I hypnotize myself with my eyes open now. I find myself in a comfortable, quiet place where I will not be disturbed so I can quietly concentrate on these words.

"I use the sound of my own voice and the power of my own imagination to deeply relax my body ... from the top of my head ... down through my feet and toes. It feels good to relax now.

"Before me I imagine a grand, ornate door on which my first name is embossed in pure, shiny gold. As I speak my name aloud (say your first name aloud) the door slowly opens all by itself, as if by some mysterious force. In addition, when I step through the threshold, I feel a deep sense of security and well-being.

"I make my way to a short stairway with five stairs that lead down into my favorite thinking place in the vast mansion. As I descend the stairs, I count backwards from five to one, and as I do, I use my imagination to relax deeper and deeper and glide into a condition of self-hypnosis, a condition of deep relaxation and heightened receptivity.

"Five ... I imagine walking down the stairs and feeling more relaxed with each number.

"Four ... the deeper I go, the more open to positive change I now become.

"Three ... effortlessly going deeper down the stairs ... feeling safe and secure.

"Two ... down into a calm and comfortable place ... where creating positive changes is effortless and uncomplicated.

"One ... at the bottom of the stairs now, and I imagine what it feels like to be in a state of self-hypnosis with my eyes open.

"I imagine entering into a welcoming reading room. I approach a plush, comfortable looking chair and sit down to relax fully. I am now hypnotized with my eyes open. I am highly suggestible in this state and remain in this deep condition while I read the suggestions pertaining to my goal.

"I easily stay hypnotized with my eyes open until I read the Wake-Up. I remain calm and focused as I begin to read the suggestions for my goal. "

(Please turn to the script of your choice.)

INSTANTLY
HYPNOTIZE OTHERS

*In the original book, I revealed how to use the
Master Induction to hypnotize others
by reading aloud and modifying
the pronouns as required.*

WHILE MANY PEOPLE HAD SUCCESS with it, I honestly found it a bit awkward to perform. The passages in the original Master Induction do not quite make sense when read to someone else. It takes too much effort to maneuver around them with different pronoun modifiers. Therefore, I have decided to create a different version so you can specifically hypnotize other people easily.

No matter the person you hypnotize, it is important they first have a basic understanding of hypnosis. Also, you need to make sure you remove any of their fears about being hypnotized. Then they will relax, participate fully, and get what they want from the session(s). To hypnotize others, follow these steps:

* Have them select a goal script they wish to work on. Bookmark that suggestion script before you begin.

* Find a place where you both will not be disturbed during the session.

* Have the person you are hypnotizing sit in a comfortable chair or sofa. You may sit across from them or sit next to them in a chair.

* Begin to read the induction below aloud. Use a soft and soothing tone of voice. Take your time between sentences and paragraphs. Pause a little where you see the three dots (...). Note: Do not read the words found in parentheses. But follow any directions they offer.

* At the end of the induction, turn to the script you have bookmarked and then continue to read. Replace the pronouns from the first person to the second person (e.g. change "I" to "You").

* Finish by reading the Wake-Up provided at the end of the script.

* Repeat the session once a day for about three to seven days until the results show.

Now you may begin to read the Modified Master Induction 2.0 script when you are ready...

"Modified Master Induction 2.0"

(to be read aloud)

"Are you ready to enjoy a relaxing hypnosis session now?" (wait for answer)

"Are you willing to follow my directions to become more successful?" (wait for answer)

"Good. Now, close your eyes, and make sure your hands and feet are uncrossed.

"As you feel a sense of privacy and comfort, let the sound of my voice soothe your mind and calm your body.

"Use your imagination and feel yourself become increasingly relaxed ... as though everything was beginning to move in slow motion ... (read slower) slow motion. Moment by moment, your mind becomes as clear as the surface of a calm and quiet mountain lake. Calm ... and quiet.

"Imagine yourself now relaxing in a small wooden boat that is gently drifting on the glassy lake. Majestic, tall trees surround the lake. The sun is shining and warms your skin. Feel its golden rays on your body, gently soothing and relaxing you from the top of your head down to the tips of your toes.

"As you imagine closing your eyes on the drifting wooden vessel, hear the leaves of the trees rustling (pause a moment to let the person hear it) and feel a refreshing breeze pass over your body (take a few seconds to let the person feel this). You smell the sweet scent of wildflowers on the wind.

"Draw a slow breath and release it. And as you do, relax twice as deeply, and let go of all stress in your body and mind ... All tension is washed away and is replaced with an incredible sense of peace and well-being, as you allow your mind and the boat to move and drift ... without a care ... along the mirror-like surface of the serene water. Just drifting now ... into gentle pathways of peace and comfort ... easily ... effortlessly ... the way you might feel on the border of a sound, deep sleep. A sound ... deep ... sleep.

"Imagine the boat has come to a gentle stop upon a lush island. You look and see that the abundant green vegetation looks well cared for. You notice a pathway that leads to a magnificent mansion. As you step out of the boat and slowly walk along the path toward the mansion, its beautiful architecture and grandeur mesmerize you.

"You come to a closed iron gate at which stands a formidable looking guard who looks at you with a steely glare. However, that glare quickly turns to a smile of recognition as the guard opens the gate and says to you 'Welcome back.' And you realize that the mansion and the island belong to you and the guard works for you.

"You walk through the gate and up to a grand, ornate door where your first name is embossed in pure gold. The door opens all by itself, as if by some mysterious force. As you step through the threshold of the door, you feel a deep sense of security and well-being. As you walk through the vast, beautifully decorated foyer, you see a large portrait of yourself looking healthy, dignified and successful.

"There are many hallways and rooms to this mansion representing the many aspects of your mind and life. But you make your way to a short stairway with five stairs that leads down into your favorite thinking place in the vast mansion.

"As you descend the stairs, you count backwards from five to one, and as you do, you use your imagination to relax deeper and to glide into a condition of hypnosis, a condition of deep relaxation and heightened receptivity.

The Manifestation Revelation

"Five ... imagine walking down the stairs and you feel more relaxed with each number.

"Four ... the deeper you go, the more open to positive change you now become.

"Three ... effortlessly going deeper down the stairs ... feeling safe and secure.

"Two ... down into a calm and comfortable place ... where creating positive change is effortless and uncomplicated.

"One ... at the bottom of the stairs now, and you imagine what it feels like to be in a deep, receptive state of hypnosis.

"You are at present highly suggestible. Every time you choose to be hypnotized in this fashion, you will go deeper and faster than the time before, because it is a relaxing wonderful experience you enjoy.

"And you can remain in this place while I now offer your subconscious mind positive and beneficial suggestions that will change your life.

"Just relax even deeper now as I continue to read to you."

(Please turn to the selected script and continue reading)

EVERYDAY SELF-HYPNOSIS

THERE IS A SIMPLE, BUT POWERFUL technique you may incorporate into your everyday routine that will get you to your goals faster than by using More Instant Self Hypnosis alone.

I wrote about it at length in my 2007 book, Self-Hypnosis Revolution: The Amazingly Simple Way to Use Self Hypnosis to Change Your Life. I will tell you about it here because it is more effective when used as a companion technique to this book.

I discovered that the things we do every day are loaded with natural symbols and lessons which, when combined with verbal suggestions, can double your life-changing results!

Here is a good way to start to understand what I mean. When you think of conventional self-hypnosis, you probably think about closing your eyes and entering a deep trance. But if you only do those techniques you are leaving out those trances you enter every day called "natural trances." Those trances can promote powerful personal growth when repeated through the various, multiple daily tasks you perform.

Natural trances are a kind of hypnosis you experience in daily life. You slip into and out of them while performing common chores like cooking, cleaning or driving. At those times, you tend to go on automatic as your brainwaves slow down into what is called the "alpha state".

I will briefly explain how you can take advantage of these natural trances as you go about your everyday routines.

How I Discovered Everyday Self-Hypnosis

It started like any other morning: I was taking my usual shower. I was becoming very relaxed as the warm water passed over my body. My mind was drifting off very pleasantly. However, instead of just humming or singing in that private moment I carried out an experiment.

It was to help me find a way to use that simple activity (showering), apply its symbolism and then rearrange it into a personal meditation (or self-talk mantra) to help me reach my goals. This "simple" idea helped me change my life even more positively over the next few months. Today it is an effective, easy habit.

The following list outlines how I achieved it—and how you can do it too:

* I attached the correct symbol to the task. I asked myself the question of what kind of symbolism showering or bathing carried. The answer was "cleansing." Then I thought about how I could create a kind of auto-suggestive mantra for that task.

* I created an appropriate autosuggestion phrase that I repeated aloud three times with emotion: *"I cleanse myself of all accumulated anger, fear and self-doubt. I cleanse myself of all accumulated anger, fear, and self-doubt. I cleanse myself of all accumulated anger, fear and self-doubt."*

* I imagined that the symbolic form of those negative emotions was like dirt leaving my body and going down the drain: Taking that shower became a symbolic ritual to cleanse my inner self!

I did this daily until I saw a change. At first, I barely noticed anything. After several days of repeating this "everyday self-hypnosis," I noticed my mood brightening and my thoughts turning more positively toward how to get what I needed/wanted in my life.

I found that when you correctly use the natural trance state—together with choosing from your daily activities and applying the power of self-suggestions based on appropriate symbols—it really pays off! Bad habits can be changed to good habits this way.

Then, I created a list of tasks-symbols-suggestions to cover most common daily activities. Here are just two examples (with hundreds more):

> *"Ironing my dress shirts became a way to use natural trance to "iron out the wrinkles in my relationships."*
>
> *"Driving to the farmer's market became a way to work on "driving myself to greater success."*

Achieving Everyday Self-hypnosis Easily—Systematically

There is nothing complicated about the Everyday Self-hypnosis technique. Here are the basics to help you better understand it:

* Select an ordinary activity

* Recognize its underlying or symbolic meaning for your life

* Create a beneficial suggestion to accompany the activity

* Recite the suggestion three times as you initiate the task

* Await the positive life changes you want

In the book, you can choose from hundreds of everyday activities you perform. You will notice that, after about a week, changes will start to manifest in your thoughts, emotions, actions and then your behavioral patterns. (For stubborn habits, please stick with this system for at least three weeks.)

Combining Techniques for Optimum Impact

You can easily combine the techniques of Everyday Self-hypnosis with minimal effort and time commitment. And it is easy to implement.

By taking advantage of working with natural trances, it takes virtually no time out of your day. All you need to do is figure out which activities you want to use when you integrate it.

To Experience Joy Each Day:

Use the "Joyful Living" script once a day for seven days. On each of those seven days, use eating as your natural trance activity. Eating carries with it the symbolism of assimilation—not only of physical nutrients but also the thoughts and ideas.

Whenever you eat repeat to yourself (aloud or silently): "I feast on joyful thoughts and attitudes."

Then, over the seven-day period, the power of those two techniques will get your subconscious to work on your goal of joyful living.

More Information is Available

If you would like more information, look over a copy of my book *Self Hypnosis Revolution: The Amazingly Simple Way to Use Self Hypnosis to Change Your Life*. It reveals the symbolic meanings of hundreds of household chores. In addition, it offers pre-written self-suggestions to design your own self-improvement program.

QUESTIONS

Do I have to read the scripts aloud?

I have received emails from users of my first book (Instant Self Hypnosis) who read the scripts silently and got excellent results. A few of my deaf readers particularly appreciated this. Still, I suggest most of you read the scripts aloud because your voice can assist the relaxation process, distract the critical factor, and intensify your results.

How many times should I perform the sessions?

Repeat your sessions once a day (for each goal on consecutive days) until you see results. Some people need only one session. For others, success happens after three to seven sessions. For a few people, it might require 21 consecutive days (because of deeply ingrained bad habits or resistant personalities). Note: some people find that twice-a-day sessions greatly accelerate their results.

Can I use multiple goal suggestion scripts each day?
Yes, but for best results please separate your sessions by several hours. For instance, you might use the "Stay in the Now" script in the morning and the "Remember Past Lives"

script in the evening. I do not recommend using more than two scripts in a single day though.

When is the best time of day to use the eyes-open method?

Choose a time when you will not be disturbed. Many people report excellent results when they use it just before bedtime. Nevertheless, any time of day will work well. Just do what is most comfortable for you.

Can I write my own suggestions for goals not included in this book?

Yes, you can write your own suggestions and I highly recommend it. In my first book, Instant Self Hypnosis, you will find helpful, detailed instructions to enable you to write your own original self-hypnosis scripts.

Why did I not feel hypnotized while I used the eyes-open method in my sessions?

You may not "feel hypnotized" because hypnosis is not a feeling. It is a self-therapy to achieve success for improving habits. In fact, trying to recognize just when you have been hypnotized can be difficult for most people. However, this method will work and here is how to tell. When positive results begin to manifest, you will have the proof you need.

Can I use this method for serious medical conditions?

No. The scripts are not a replacement for professional, medical, or psychological advice and treatment.

Can I record the scripts and play them back to get the same results?

Yes, you may read the scripts into a recording device and play them back. However, keep in mind that you are changing the eyes-open method of hypnosis, and your attention might wander or you might fall asleep while listening to the audios. My hypnosis-as-you-read method gets you more involved. Listening to a hypnosis recording takes less effort than reading a script aloud, and that effort is exactly what makes the eyes-open method more effective for many people—because you are involved. Many people report that listening to the hypnosis mp3s and reading the corresponding script (induction and suggestion) generates twice the positive effect!

ABOUT

Forbes Robbins Blair is a professional hypnosis therapist, author, manifestation coach and entrepreneur. He considers it a privilege to share what he knows about manifestation with his readers and students.

He has written multiple books about eyes open self-hypnosis including his first, *Instant Self Hypnosis: How to Hypnotize Yourself with Your Eyes Open* (amzn.to/1ymUvxu).

He began teaching his innovative self-hypnosis methods in 1997 and has appeared on national and regional radio and television for his expertise.

He is also a long-time student and practitioner of all things metaphysical which includes manifestation and the Higher Self.

He also produces eBooks and multimedia programs about the Law of Attraction and self-growth.

If you have any questions or need to reach Forbes, you are welcome to reach him here:

Visit his website here:
http://www.forbesrobbinsblair.com

Contact him by email here:
webmaster@forbesrobbinsblair.com

REVIEW

If you enjoyed this book, I would really appreciate it if you would write a customer review. That would let the world know how it helped you. Thank you.
　Please review this book here (amzn.to/1MeDHw6)

BOOKS+

Self-Hypnosis Books:

INSTANT SELF HYPNOSIS:
How to Hypnotize Yourself
with Your Eyes Open

Stop smoking, lose weight, and stop stressing out. In his original bestselling book, Forbes Robbins Blair reveals his remarkable method that allows you to hypnotize yourself as you read. This bestselling international classic contains 35 powerful scripts to improve your life in practical ways. You will us this book repeatedly. Here is the link: http://www.amazon.com/Instant-Self-Hypnosis-Hypnotize-Yourself-Your-ebook/dp/B00348UMQM

SELF HYPNOSIS REVOLUTION:
The Amazingly Simple Way to Use
Self Hypnosis to Change Your Life

Learn how everyday tasks can be used with the power of suggestion to create remarkable transformations in five key areas of your life.

This innovative autosuggestion method is easy, fun and takes no extra time out of your day. Here is the link: http://www.amazon.com/Self-Hypnosis-Revolution-Amazingly-Simple-Change/dp/1402206704

SELF HYPNOSIS AS YOU READ:
42 Life Changing Scripts

Forbes' fourth self-hypnosis book, it includes the scripts: "Lose the Last 10 Pounds," "Never Be Late Again," "Save More Money." This book contains multiple scripts to induce hypnosis with the eyes-open method, as well as advanced material never published before.

It includes multiple inductions and lots of new scripts as well. Not to mention, there are some powerful tips, techniques, and stories throughout. Some readers say it is his best self-hypnosis book. Here is the link: http://www.amazon.com/Self-Hypnosis-As-You-Read-ebook/dp/B00FRK2Y4S

Manifestation Books:

THE MANIFESTATION MANIFESTO:
Amazing Technique and Strategies to Attract the Life You Want— No Visualization Required

The first book in Forbes Robbins Blair's Amazing Manifestation Strategy series, creates a contract with your inner self to create the life you want. It's loaded with over 20 manifestation techniques. You learn to emphasize what you want to attract. You'll repel negativity. See why this book became an Amazon bestseller. Here is the link: https://www.amazon.com/Manifestation-Manifesto-Techniques-Strategies-Visualization-ebook/dp/B00LY7ZBQG

THE MANIFESTATION MATRIX:
Nine Steps to Manifest Money, Success and Love When Asking and Believing Are Not Working

The second in the Amazing Manifestation Strategies series, this book provides an easy, powerful systematic formula for manifesting whatever you want. It contains clear and practical steps which only take an hour to make it work right away. Here is the link: http://www.amazon.com/Manifestation-Matrix-Manifest-Believing-Strategies-ebook/dp/B00UB49HBS

THE MANIFESTATION MINDSET:
How to Think Like A True Manifestor and Overcome the Doubts Blocking Your Success

Is doubt blocking you from manifesting the life you want? Whether you are trying to attract money, a life partner or abundant health, this third book in the Amazing Manifestation Strategies series reveals nine ways to transform from a mere dabbler into a true manifestor.

With this book, you will start to see a radical shift in your thoughts and behavior; and, you will be transformed into a manifestation powerhouse! Here is the link:
https://www.amazon.com/Manifestation-Mindset-Manifestor-Overcome-Strategies/dp/1522795421

THE MANIFESTATION REVELATION:
How to Align with Your Higher Self to Manifest, Balance, Happiness, and Prosperity

Reach the next level of manifestation power with your higher self! Without a masterful understanding of its laws, your intentions can bring unfortunate consequences. Though this subject can be confusing and complex, Forbes makes the Higher Self easy to understand.

Filled with extraordinary story lessons and uniquely effective strategies, you'll learn to attract the best life offers.

Includes why understanding the higher self is the most important aspect of the law of Attraction, how cosmic cycles can help laser-target your goals. Includes the Tower of Light meditation which is uplifting and deeply effective and the steps and strategies to realize your dreams.

In this fourth book in Forbes Robbins Blair's bestselling Amazing Manifestation Strategies series, you'll learn about your incredible ally and how to access your Higher Self to manifest a better life. Go here to look inside The Manifestation Revelation (amzn.to/2fkB7xR)

THE MANIFESTATION TRILOGY:
Manifest the Life You Want with Focus, Clarity, and Balance

Three Best-selling Manifestation Books-In-One!

Become more successful with the law of attraction with this practical 3-in-1 compilation. Make the most of the ancient principles of the Law of Attraction with this guide. Here is an overview:

* **Book #1, The Manifestation Manifesto,** introduces you to the subject of manifestation and contains over 20 excellent strategies to get what you want

without the need to visualize anything. It's good for beginners and seasoned manifestors alike. It's full of secrets to rid yourself of possible mental and emotional obstacles to harness your startling manifestation mind power.

*** Book #2, The Manifestation Matrix,** offers an easy, multi-step manifestation formula anyone may use to attain just about any realistic goal, including money, love, and career success. However, it's not only about the formula. It helps you learn how to focus your mind on what you want. It teaches how to channel your manifestation power constructively. It contains ideas not common in other manifestation books. You will also learn why these ideas are valuable.

*** Book #3, The Manifestation Mindset,** takes you from a person who merely dabbles with manifestation to a person who truly lives it. This book centers around nine powerful manifestation strategies, which include specific and effective experiments to help affirm your belief in your power and get rid of doubt that stands in your way. Also, featured: "The Manifestation Powerhouse Meditation," which helps you program your mind to radiate your desires to the Universe.

Here are a few of Trilogy's 33 highlights:

* life-changing meditations that reprogram your mind for success

* how to identify and change beliefs that block manifestation

* why your vision board failed and an easy, unique way to fix it

* 9 ways to collect Vital Energy (chi, prana) to manifest things faster

* ways to recognize your manifestation power with symbols and affirmations

* an easy way to stimulate your heart chakra

* improve the quality of what you manifest

* two magic words that put you in an energetic receiving state

* five mini-experiments you can perform to prove your manifestation ability

* the mental law that can ruin your success, and how to overcome it

* how to use a "magic manifestation talisman"

* and over a dozen more

With this 3-in-1 book, best-selling self-hypnosis and manifestation author Forbes Robbins Blair shares what has worked for him and thousands of his readers. Allow his effective, original strategies to work for you. Look inside The Manifestation Trilogy here: (amzn.to/2kxqZ8l)

Other Products:

THE GENIE WITHIN:
Your Wish is Granted

Based on classes Mr. Blair taught in the Baltimore-Washington DC area, this eBook and Mp3 audio course teaches you how to use your creative imagination to manifest your wishes. And it is fun, innovative, and easy to do. Here is the link: http://www.forbesrobbinsblair.com/geniewithin.html

Attract Surplus Money Mp3

This high-quality self-hypnosis audio is based on a script from the book *More Instant Self Hypnosis*. This bestselling hypnotic audio Mp3 programs your mind to attract more money. Soothing and effective, you can download and listen to it right now. Here is the link for it: ttp://www.forbesrobbinsblair.com/store/p17/Attract_Wealth_hypnosis_mp3.html

SOUL OF THE KNIGHT:
Awaken the Warrior Within

Tap into your inner confidence, discipline, and motivation as you connect with the noble Knight within. This eBook/audio Mp3 program is like nothing else. If you are drawn to the image of medieval Knights, this program can help you transform your life quickly and dramatically. Mr. Blair believes it is the most powerful product he has ever produced.

Here is the link: http://www.forbesrobbinsblair.com/soul-of-the-knight.html

Positive Living Store

Forbes Robbins Blair's online store includes all his original products including courses, eBooks, and audio mp3s which are not for sale anywhere else. You can get more explanation by going to his online store.

Here is the link to Forbes' Positive Living Store: http://www.forbesrobbinsblair.com/store/c1/Featured_Products.html

THANK YOU

Thank you for taking the time to read *The Manifestation Revelation*. I am fortunate and honored to share with you these strategies about the Higher Self and its relationship to manifestation.

If you enjoyed this book, would you do me a favor and write a customer review at amazon.com? Just tell people what you liked about it. Your opinion really makes a difference.

NOTES

NOTES

Made in the USA
Las Vegas, NV
19 September 2025